Guiding Those Left Behind
In New York

LEGAL AND PRACTICAL THINGS
YOU NEED TO DO
TO SETTLE AN ESTATE IN NEW YORK

and

HOW TO ARRANGE YOUR OWN AFFAIRS
TO AVOID UNNECESSARY COSTS
TO YOUR FAMILY

By AMELIA E. POHL, ESQ.

and New York Attorney
VINCENT J. RUSSO

EAGLE PUBLISHING COMPANY OF BOCA

EAGLE PUBLISHING COMPANY OF BOCA
4199 N. Dixie Highway, #2
Boca Raton, FL   33431   E-mail: info@eaglepublishing.com

Printed in the United States of America
ISBN 1932464115
Library of Congress Catalog Card Number 2005902775

Guiding Those Left Behind In New York

CONTENTS

About The Book

We tried to make this book as comprehensive as possible so there are specialized sections of the book that do not apply to the general population and may not be of interest to you. The following GUIDE POSTS appear throughout the book. You can read the section if the situation applies to you or skip the section if it doesn't. Skipping the section will not affect the continuity of the book.

GUIDE POSTS

The SPOUSE POST means that the information provided is specifically for the spouse of the decedent. If the decedent was single, you can skip this section.

The CALL-A-LAWYER POST alerts you to a situation that may require the assistance of an attorney. See the end of this chapter for information about how to find a lawyer.

The CAUTION POST alerts you to a potential problem. It is followed by a suggestion about how to avoid the problem.

The SPECIAL SITUATION POST means that the information given in that paragraph applies to a particular event or situation; for example when the decedent dies a violent death. If the situation does not apply, you can skip the section.

The Organization of the Book

Guiding Those Left Behind refers to the things that need to be done in order to settle an Estate in New York. The purpose of this book is to guide the reader through that process. It explains:

1. How to tend to the funeral and burial
2. What agencies need to be notified
3. How to locate the decedent's property
4. What bills need (and do not need) to be paid
5. How to determine who is entitled to inherit the decedent's property
6. How to transfer the decedent's property to the proper beneficiary

We devoted a chapter to each of these 6 steps; and for those who are in charge of settling an Estate, we placed a CHECK LIST at the end of Chapter 6 summarizing things that need to be done. Once you read Chapters 1 through 6 you will be able to identify those problems that can happen when someone dies. Using those Chapters as a base, you can set up your own Estate Plan so that your family is not burdened by similar problems. The rest of the book (Chapters 7, 8 and 9) suggests different methods you can use to accomplish this goal.

GLOSSARY

This book is designed for the average reader. Legal terminology has been kept to a minimum. There is a glossary at the end of the book in the event you come across a legal term that is not familiar to you.

FICTITIOUS NAMES AND EVENTS

The examples in this book are based loosely on actual events; however, all names are fictitious; and the events, as portrayed, are fictitious.

Reading the Law

Where applicable, we identified the state statute or federal statute that is the basis of the discussion. We did this as a reference, and also to encourage the general public to read the law as it is written. Prior to the Internet the only way you could look up the law was to physically take yourself to the local courthouse law library or the law section of a public library. Today all of the state and federal statutes are literally at your finger tips. They are just a mouse click away on the Internet. To look up the law all you need is the address of the Web site and the identifying number of the statute.

FEDERAL STATUTES
http://www4.law.cornell.edu/uscode

NEW YORK STATUTES
http://assembly.state.ny.us/ALIS

New York has consolidated their laws into 111 titles that are listed alphabetically, such as

Abandoned Property Law ("Aband. Prop.")
Civil Practice Law and Rules ("C.P.L.R")
Domestic Relations Law ("Dom. Rel.")
Estates, Powers & Trusts Law ("Est. Powers & Trusts")
Executive Law ("Exec.")
General Obligations Law ("Gen. Oblig.")
Insurance Law ("Insur.")
Public Health Law ("Pub. Health")
Social Services Law ("Social Services")
Surrogate's Court Procedure Act ("Surr. Ct. Proc. Act")
Worker's Compensation Law ("Work Comp.")

Each title is divided into numbered sections. To look up a statute, go to the Web site, find the title, and then the section within the title. You may find it both interesting and profitable to read the law as it is actually written, if you come across a topic that is important to you.

Vincent J. Russo, Esq.

VINCENT J. RUSSO is a founding member, Fellow and past president of the National Academy of Elder Law Attorneys. He is a founding member and past chair of the Elder Law Section of the New York State Bar Association and is a member of the American Bar Association. He is past chair and founder of the Legal Advisory Committee to the Alzheimer's Assoc. Long Island Chapter, a member of the committees on Elder Law of the Nassau and Suffolk County Bar Associations, chair of the Guardianship Committee as well as a former Board member of the United Cerebral Palsy Association of Nassau County.

VINCENT J. RUSSO is nationally recognized for his contribution and achievements in the field of Elder Law. Vincent is the managing shareholder of the law firm of Vincent J. Russo & Associates, P.C. of Westbury and Islandia, NY.

Vincent earned his law degree from Fordham University School of Law and a Masters of Law in Taxation from the Boston University of Law. He is admitted to the New York, Massachusetts and Florida State Bar Associations, and is a certified Elder Law attorney by the National Elder Law Foundation.

Mr. Russo is the co-founder of the Theresa Alessandra Russo Foundation established in the memory of his daughter, Teresa. The Foundation supports Art For All Children by granting funds for recreational programs for children with disabilities.

As a noted authority, author and lecturer in Elder Law, Mr. Russo has championed the rights of the elderly since 1985. He is a nationally recognized author, lecturer and authority in Elder Law. Vincent J. Russo is a frequent speaker at the Joint Conference on Law and Aging in Washington, DC. He has been keynote speaker at the Annual Conferences of the American Institute of Certified Public Accountants, the National Association of Professional Geriatric Care Managers, and the New Jersey Bar Association.

Vincent J. Russo has been the special guest on many radio and television programs, including CNN, NBC'S TODAY SHOW, CNBC, THE FOX NEWS NETWORK, CSPAN II and NEWS 12 LONG ISLAND.

Vincent J. Russo is the co-author of *New York Elder Law Practice* as well as Consulting Attorney for *When Someone Dies In New York*.

Mr. Russo has published numerous articles concerning the elderly and their families which have appeared in the New York State Bar Journal, the NAELA Quarterly, the New York State Queens County Bar Journal, the Long Island Examiner, ELDERCARE, a newsletter published by Eldercare, Ltd., the Elderlaw Report, Shepherd's Elder Care/ Law Newsletter, Personal Advantage/Financial published by Boardroom Reports, Inc.

A person with strong family values, Vincent makes his home in Lido Beach, NY with his wife Susan and their children.

For an illustration of some of Vincent's published materials, as well as his guest appearance on the "NBC Today Show" and other facets of his leadership in Elder Law, visit his Web site at: www.russoelderlaw.com.

Amelia E. Pohl, Esq.

Before becoming an attorney in 1985, AMELIA E. POHL taught mathematics on both the high school and college level. During her tenure as Associate Professor of Mathematics at Prince George's Community College in Maryland, she wrote several books including

Probability: A Set Theory Approach
Principals of Counting
Common Stock Sense.

During her practice of law Attorney Pohl observed that many people want to reduce the high cost of legal fees by performing or assisting with their own legal transactions. Attorney Pohl found that, with a bit of guidance, people are able to perform many legal transactions for themselves. Attorney Pohl utilizes her background as teacher, author and attorney to provide that "bit of guidance" to the general public in the form of self-help legal books that she has written. Amelia E. Pohl is currently "translating" this book for the remaining 49 states:

Guiding Those Left Behind in Maine
Guiding Those Left Behind In North Dakota
Guiding Those Left Behind In Wyoming, etc.

SPECIAL THANKS

Many people contributed to the development of this book. We wish to give special thanks to CHARLES B. BARON, an attorney with the law firm of Vincent J. Russo & Associates, P.C., for his assistance, encouragement and support.

THE DESIGN ARTIST

LUBOSH CECH designed the cover of this book. He is a renowned artist, with extensive educational background and professional work experience. He studied design, applied art, and painting in his native Prague, Czech Republic. He also studied at the University of Bologna in Italy. Since moving to the United States in 1984, Mr. Cech has been designing art exhibitions, working as an art director, and graphic designer. Mr. Cech is a photographer and often incorporates his photographs into his art work.

Lubosh Cech is the founder of OKO DESIGN STUDIO located in Portland, Oregon. For more information about Mr. Cech and the OKO Design Studio visit his Web site.
http://www.okodesignstudio.com

THE PHOTOGRAPHER

The photograph that appears on the cover was taken by photographer GENE OSON.

ACKNOWLEDGMENT

When someone dies, the family attorney is often among the first to be called. Family members have questions about whether probate is necessary, who to notify, how to get possession of the assets, etc. Over the years, as we practiced in the field of Elder Law, we noticed that the questions raised were much the same family to family. We both agreed that a book answering such questions would be of service to the general public.

We also observed, that those who had experience in settling the estate of a loved one were more understanding of the process, and better able to make decisions about how to arrange their own finances to avoid problems that could arise in settling an estate. We named the book *Guiding Those Left Behind*. The "Guiding" refers to the guidance that this book gives in the event that you need to settle the Estate of your loved one. It also refers to the guidance that you can give to your family by setting up your own Estate Plan so that your family is not burdened by unnecessary costs and delays in settling your estate.

We wish to thank all of the clients, whom we have had the honor and pleasure to serve, for providing us with the impetus to produce this book.

When You Need A Lawyer

The purpose of the book is to give the reader a basic understanding of what needs to be done when someone dies, and to provide information about how a person can arrange his own affairs to avoid problems for his own family. It is not intended as a substitute for legal counsel or any other kind of professional advice. If you have any legal question, you should seek the counsel of an attorney. When looking for an attorney, consider three things: EXPERTISE, COST and PERSONALITY.

EXPERTISE

The state of New York does not have a program to certify that an attorney is specialized in a particular area of law. However, attorneys are allowed to state that they are certified by an accredited institution, if such is the case. For example, the National Elder Law Foundation has a certification program for the field of Elder Law. An attorney certified by the Foundation, or other program such as being a Chartered Estate Planning Practitioner is allowed to make that fact known to the public.

The New York State Bar Association has a Lawyer Referral & Information Service ("LRIS"). They will refer you to an attorney in your area who practices the type of law that you seek. You can reach LRIS (800) 342-3661, or visit the New York State Bar Web site.

 NEW YORK STATE BAR ASSOCIATION
http://www.nysba.org

New York City has its own Lawyer Referral Service. You can call them at (212) 626-7373, or visit their Web site.

 THE ASSOC. OF THE BAR OF THE CITY OF NEW YORK
http://abcny.org

One of the most reliable ways to find an attorney is through personal referral. Ask your friends, family or business acquaintances if they used an attorney for the field of law that you seek and whether they were pleased with the results. It is important to employ an attorney who is experienced in the area of law you seek. Your friend may have a wonderful Estate Planning attorney, but if you suffered an injury to your body, then you need an attorney who is experienced in Personal Injury.

Before employing an attorney for a job, ask how long he has practiced that type of law and what percentage of his practice is devoted to that type of law.

COST

In addition to the attorney's experience, it is important to check what it will cost in attorney's fees. When you call for an appointment ask what the attorney will charge for the initial consultation and the approximate cost for the service you seek. Ask whether there will be additional costs such as filing fees, accounting fees, expert witness fees, etc.

If the least expensive attorney is out of your price range then you can call your local county Bar Association for the telephone number of the Legal Aid office nearest you or you can call LRIS at (800) 342-3661.

The American Bar Association has a listing of State Legal Service Organizations at the Pro Bono section of its Web site.

 THE AMERICAN BAR ASSOCIATION
http://www.abanet.org

PERSONALITY

Of equal importance to the attorney's experience and legal fees, is your relationship with the attorney. How easy was it to reach the attorney? Did you go through layers of receptionists and legal assistants before being allowed to speak to the attorney? Did the attorney promptly return your call? If you had difficulty reaching the attorney, then you can expect similar problems should you employ that attorney.

Did the attorney treat you with respect? Did the attorney treat you paternally with a "father knows best" attitude or did he treat you as an intelligent person with the ability to understand the options available to you and the ability to make your own decision based on the information provided to you?

Are you able to understand and easily communicate with the attorney? Is he speaking to you in plain English or is his explanation of the matter so full of legalese to be almost meaningless to you?

Do you find the attorney's personality to be pleasant or grating? Sometimes people rub each other the wrong way. It is like rubbing a cat the wrong way. Stroking a cat from head to tail is pleasing to the cat, but petting it in the opposite direction, no matter how well intended, causes friction. If the lawyer makes you feel annoyed or uncomfortable, then find another attorney.

It is worth the effort to take the time to interview as many attorneys as it takes to find one with the right expertise, fee schedule and personality for you.

The First Week 1

Dealing with the death of a close family member or friend is difficult. Not only do you need to deal with your own emotions, but often with those of your family and friends. Sometimes their sorrow is more painful to you, than what you are experiencing yourself.

In addition to the emotional impact of a death, there are many things that need to be done, from arranging the funeral and burial, to closing out the business affairs of the *decedent* (the person who died) and finally giving whatever property is left to the proper beneficiary.

The funeral and burial take only a few days. Wrapping up the affairs of the decedent may take considerably longer. This chapter explains what things you (the spouse or closest family member) need to do during the first week, beginning at the moment of death and continuing through the funeral.

  MALE GENDER USED

Rather than use "he/she" or "his/her" for simplicity
(and hoping not to offend anyone)
we will refer to the decedent and his
Personal Representative using the male gender.

References to other people will be in both genders.

AUTOPSIES

In today's high tech world of medicine, doctors are fairly certain of the cause of death, but if there is a question, the family may be asked permission to perform an autopsy. If, during his lifetime, the decedent appointed a *Health Care Agent* (someone to make his medical decisions), he can authorize the examination. If no Agent was appointed, the surviving spouse or a next of kin may consent; however no autopsy may be performed if a relative or friend objects because it is against the decedent's religious belief (Pub. Health 4210-C).

The person who authorizes the autopsy must agree to pay for it because the cost of the examination is not covered under most health insurance plans. And that cost could be sizeable, running anywhere from several hundred to several thousand dollars, but it may be in the family's best interest to consent to the autopsy. The examination might reveal a genetic disorder that could be treated if it later appears in another family member. Death from a car "accident" could have been a heart attack at the wheel. Perhaps the patient who died suddenly in a hospital was misdiagnosed. The nursing home resident could have died from negligence and not old age. Even if none of these are found, knowing the cause of death with certainty is better than not knowing.

That was the case with the family of a woman who was taken to the hospital complaining of stomach pains. The doctors thought she might be suffering from gallbladder disease, but she died before they could effectively treat her. A doctor suggested that an autopsy be performed to determine the exact cause of death. The woman had three daughters, one of whom objected to the autopsy: "Why spend that kind of money? It won't bring Mom back."

The daughter's wishes were respected, however over the years as they aged and became ill with their own various ailments, they would undergo physical examinations. As part of taking their medical history, doctors routinely asked "And what was the cause of your mother's death?"

None could answer the question.

This is not a dramatic story. No mysterious genetic disorder ever occurred in any of her daughters, nor in any of their children. But each daughter (including the one who objected) at some point in her life, was confronted with the nagging question "What did Mom die of?"

AUTOPSIES PERFORMED BY CORONER

When a person dies, a physician must sign a medical certification stating the cause of death. This is not a problem if a person dies in a hospital or nursing home from natural causes. If the person dies at home and the death was expected, the treating physician can be contacted to sign the medical certificate verifying that the decedent died of natural causes. But if a person dies, suddenly, at home, and he was not under the care of a physician, whoever discovers the body must call 911 to summon the police. The law enforcement officer will call the Coroner or Medical Examiner to determine the cause of death (County Law 674 (3a)).

If the death occurred under questionable circumstances your family can request that the County conduct the autopsy. If the Medical Examiner agrees, there will be no charge to the decedent's family or to his Estate. However, if that is not an option, and the family wants an autopsy, then whoever authorizes the procedure must agree to be responsible for payment.

Under New York law, an autopsy is mandatory under certain circumstances. The Coroner or Medical Examiner will order an autopsy in each of the following cases:

⇨ it is essential to the investigation of a homicide

⇨ any death that may pose an immediate and substantial threat to the public (Pub. Health 4210-c)

⇨ when the decedent was an inmate of a correctional facility, regardless of whether the death occurred within the facility (County Law 674).

The Coroner or Medical Examiner will order an autopsy in all of these circumstances. Once the Medical Examiner takes possession of a body, it will not be released until the examination is complete. Meanwhile, the family can proceed with arrangements for the funeral. The funeral director will contact the Coroner or Medical Examiner to determine when he can pick up the body and proceed with the funeral arrangements.

AUTOPSIES PERFORMED BY THE INSURANCE COMPANY

A company that issues an accident or health insurance policy in New York is required to include a statement in the policy that the company has the right to perform an autopsy (Insurance 3216(c)(14d)). The cost of the autopsy must be paid for by the insurance company, so they will not order an autopsy unless there is some important reason to do so.

ANATOMICAL GIFTS

Early on in the donor program those over 65 were not considered as suitable candidates. Today, however, the condition of the organ, and not the age, is the determining factor. Hospital personnel determine whether a mortally ill patient is a candidate for an organ donation, and if so, they will contact the local Organ Procurement Organization (Pub. Health 4351).

The federal government has established regional Organ Procurement Organizations throughout the United States to coordinate the donor program. There are five Organ Procurement Organizations that service New York. The Center for Donation and Transplant (Eastern New York), The Center for Organ Recovery & Education (Chemung County), New York Organ Donor Network, Inc. (Southeast New York), Upstate New York Transplant Services, Inc. (Western New York), Finger Lakes Donor Recovery Network (Central New York).

The Organization, together with the doctor who is treating the patient, will determine whether the patient is a suitable donor.

GIFT AUTHORIZED PRIOR TO DEATH
If, before death, the decedent made an anatomical gift by signing a donor card, the hospital personnel or the donor's doctor need to be made aware of the gift in quick proximity to the time of death — preferably before death. If it is determined that the donation is medically acceptable, the gift will be made. No family member need give permission, provided the hospital has a copy of the decedent's unrevoked donor card.

GIFT AUTHORIZED BY THE FAMILY

If no donor card is on record, and it is determined that the decedent is a suitable donor, someone who is specially trained will approach the family to request permission for the donation. New York statute states an order of priority for those who can give permission:

1st	spouse	2nd	adult son or daughter
3rd	either parent	4th	adult brother or sister
5th	court appointed Guardian, if any.		

Every effort must be made to contact those people with highest priority. No gift can be made if someone with higher priority objects. For example, if the sister of the decedent agrees to the gift (4th in priority) and the decedent had an adult child (2nd in priority), the child needs to be made aware of the gift. If the child objects, no gift can be made. Similarly, the statute prohibits the gift is contrary to the decedent's religious belief, or if prior to death, he ever expressed an objection to such donation (Pub. Health 4351).

AFTER THE DONATION

Once the donation is made the body is delivered to the funeral home and prepared for burial or cremation as directed by the family. The donation does not disfigure the body so there can be an open casket viewing if the family so wishes. Some regional Organ Procurement Organizations have an aftercare program that includes a letter of condolence to the family and an expression of gratitude for the gift. For privacy reasons, the identity of the recipient of the gift is not disclosed, but on request from the family, the local Organ Procurement Organization will give the family basic demographic information about the donation, such as the age, sex, marital status, number of children and occupation of the recipient of the gift.

CAVEAT: Federal law prohibits payment for organ donations (42 U.S.C. 274 e). There is no ban on payments made to prepare organs or tissue for transplantation, nor is there any ban on charges made to transport bodies or body parts. Not-for-profit, as well as for-profit, companies have sprung up that are in the business of preparing and delivering body parts. These companies request donations from families — so they are not violating federal law by paying for the donation. The company prepares the body tissue or other parts of the donated body, and then distributes the parts throughout the United States to physicians, hospitals, research centers, etc. In many cases, the monies charged for preparation and transportation includes a sizable profit.

If a company or organization other than your local Organ Procurement Organization approaches you to make a donation, before agreeing, you may want to learn about the company that is making the request.

> *What is the name of the company?*
> *Where are their main headquarters located?*
> *What is their primary business activity?*
> *What is the name and job description of the*
> *person making the request?*

DETERMINE THE END USE OF THE DONATION

You may want to ask what they intend to do with the tissue or body part. If it is being used for research, then what type of research? Where is the research being conducted? If it will be used for transplantation, then what agency (doctor, hospital) will receive the donation and where is that agency located?

Once you have this information you can make an informed decision as to whether you wish to make the donation to that organization.

GIFT FOR EDUCATION OR RESEARCH

Consider offering to release the body for the purpose of education or research in the event that the decedent signed a donor card, but was not an appropriate candidate for an organ donation. You can offer to release the body to a school of medicine at a university for the purpose of education or research.

Some schools that currently accept donations are:
State University of New York   (315) 464-5120
Upstate Medical Center; Dept. of Anatomy
Syracuse, NY   13210

State University of NY at Stony Brook   (631) 444-3111
Health Science Center; Dept. of Anatomical Sciences
Stony Brook, NY   11794

Cornell University Medical College   (212) 746-5677
Dept. of Anatomy and Cell Biology
New York, NY   10021

You need to call the school within 24 hours of the death to determine whether they will accept the body. They will not accept bodies that weigh more than 300 pounds or have died from a contagious disease or from crushing injuries. Many schools pay for the cost of local transportation. You need to inquire whether the school will pay for the cost of transporting the body to the facility.

The study can take up to two years to complete. At the end of the study the remains are cremated. The *cremains* (cremated remains) will be placed in a cemetery that is local to the university; or if the family wishes, the cremains will be delivered to the next of kin.

THE FUNERAL

Approximately ten percent of deaths occur suddenly because of accident, suicide, foul play or undetected illness. But, in general, death occurs after a lengthy illness, with a common scenario being that of an aged person who dies after being ill for several months, if not years. In such case, family and friends are prepared for the happening. Expected or not, the first job is the disposition of the body.

THE PREARRANGED FUNERAL

Increasingly, people are arranging, in advance, for their own funeral and burial. This makes it easier on the family both financially and emotionally. All the decisions have been made and there is no guessing what the decedent would have wanted.

If the decedent made provision for his burial, you should come across a cemetery deed or perhaps a certificate for a burial plot. If he made provision for his funeral, you should find a PRENEED FUNERAL PLAN. You need to read the contract to determine what provisions were made. If the Plan was paid by installments, you need to determine whether it is paid in full. You also need to determine whether the contract was a fixed price agreement or whether there will be additional charges.

If you cannot locate the contract, but you know the decedent made provision for his funeral and burial, call the funeral home and ask them to send you a copy of the contract. If you believe the decedent purchased a Preneed Funeral Plan but you do not know the name of the funeral home, then call the local funeral homes. Many local funeral homes are owned by national firms with computer capacity to identify people who have purchased a contract at any of their many locations.

Once you have possession of the Agreement, take it with you to the funeral home and go over the terms of the Agreement with the funeral director. Inquire whether there will be any charge that is not included in the contract.

MAKING FUNERAL ARRANGEMENTS

If the decedent died unexpectedly or without having made any prior funeral arrangements, then your first job is to choose a funeral director and make arrangements for the funeral or cremation. Most people choose the nearest or most conveniently located funeral home without comparison shopping. However prices for these services can vary significantly from funeral home to funeral home. Savings can be had if you take the time to make a few phone calls.

Receiving price quotes by telephone is your right under Federal law. Federal Trade Commission ("FTC") Rule 453.2 (b) (1) requires a funeral director to give an accurate telephone quote of the prices of his goods and services. Funeral homes are listed in the telephone directory under FUNERAL DIRECTORS. If you live in a small town, there may be only one or two listings. If such is the case, then check out some funeral homes in the next largest city.

Funeral directors usually provide the following services:
➢ arrange for the transportation of the body
   to the funeral home and then to the burial site
➢ obtain burial transit permits
➢ arrange for the embalming or cremation of the body
➢ arrange funeral and memorial services
   and the viewing of the body
➢ obtain information for the death certificate
➢ order copies of the death certificate for the family
➢ have memorial cards printed.

To compare prices you will need to determine:

✧ what is included in the price of a basic funeral plan

✧ whether you can expect any additional cost.

It may be necessary to have the body embalmed if you are going to have a viewing. Embalming is not necessary if you order a direct cremation or an immediate burial without a viewing. Federal Trade Commission Rule 453.5 prohibits the funeral home from charging an embalming fee unless you order the service.

If the decedent did not own a burial space, then that cost must be included when making funeral arrangements.

PURCHASING THE CASKET

When comparison-shopping, you will find that the single most expensive item in the funeral arrangement is the casket. Most funeral directors will quote you a price for a basic funeral plan that does not include the cost of the casket. Directors usually quote a range of prices for the casket, saying that you will need to come in and choose the casket at the time you contract for the funeral.

When selecting a casket you need to be aware that there may be a considerable mark-up in the price quoted by the funeral director. You do not need to go "sole source" when purchasing the casket. You can purchase the casket elsewhere and have it delivered to the funeral home to be used instead of the one offered by the funeral director. Funeral homes are required to accept caskets purchased elsewhere, and they may not charge a handling fee for accepting that casket. But if the price list given to you by the funeral home states that the price of their casket includes a specific dollar amount for basic services, then the funeral director is allowed to add that dollar amount to the charge for his services, should you purchase the casket elsewhere (FTC Rule 453.2, 453.4).

Caskets are not usually displayed for sale in a shopping mall, so most of us have no idea of the going price for a casket. With the advent of the Internet, you can learn all about the cost of any item, even a casket, by using your search engine to find a retail casket sales dealer. If you are not computer literate, you can locate the nearest retail casket sales outlet by looking in the yellow pages under CASKETS. You may need to look in the telephone directory for the nearest large city to find a listing. By making a call to a retail casket sales dealer, you will become knowledgeable in the price range of caskets. You can then decide what is a reasonable price for the product you seek.

The best time to do your comparison shopping is before you go to the funeral home to arrange for the funeral. Once you have determined what you should pay for the casket, it is only fair to give the funeral director the opportunity to meet that price. If you cannot reach a meeting of the minds, then you can always order the casket from the retail sales dealer and have it delivered to the funeral home.

ON-LINE FUNERAL SERVICES

The Internet is changing the way the world does business, and the funeral industry is no exception. A growing number of mortuaries are offering live Webcasts of funerals and wakes for those who are unable to pay their respects in person.

There are Web sites where you can post an obituary. There are on-line memorial chat rooms as well as on-line eulogies and testimonials. There is even a Web site that offers a posthumous e-mail service which allows people to leave final messages for friends and relatives. You can locate these services using your favorite search engine and typing in "obituaries."

THE CREMATION

Increasingly people are opting for cremation. Based on statistics published by the CREMATION ASSOCIATION OF NORTH AMERICA, over 23% of those who die each year in New York are cremated. That percentage is growing. The reasons for choosing cremation are varied, but for the majority, it is a matter of finances. The cost of cremation is approximately one-sixth that of an ordinary funeral and burial. A major saving is the cost of the casket. No casket is necessary for the cremation and Federal law prohibits a Funeral Director from saying that a casket is required for a direct cremation (FTC Rule 453.3 (b)ii). You may need a suitable container to deliver the body to the crematory. After the cremation, you will need an urn for the ashes.

If you are having a memorial service in a place of worship and no viewing of the body before the cremation, consider contracting with a facility that does cremations only. Look in the telephone book under CREMATION SERVICES. You will also see cremation "societies" in the telephone book. Some are for-profit and others non-profit. You can also find advertisements for cremation services on the Internet.

THE DECEDENT WITH A PACEMAKER
Cremating a body with a pacemaker or any radiation producing device can cause damage to the cremation chamber or to the person performing the cremation. Every body delivered for cremation must be accompanied by a statement from a physician, Coroner or Medical Examiner certifying that the body does not contain a battery or power cell (Pub. Health 4202). If the decedent was wearing such devise, you need to arrange to have it removed.

THE OVERWEIGHT DECEDENT

If the decedent weighs more than 300 pounds, then you need to check to see if the Cremation service has facilities large enough to handle the body. If you cannot locate a crematory that can accommodate the body, you will need to make burial arrangements.

DISPOSING OF THE CREMAINS

If the cremains are to be placed in a cemetery, you need to obtain a suitable urn for the burial. The container provided by the crematory can be used, or you can purchase an urn from the funeral director or crematory service director. Urns cost much less than caskets, but they can cost several hundred dollars. You may wish to do some comparison shopping by calling a retail sales casket dealer.

Many cemeteries have a separate building called a *columbarium*, which is especially designed to store urns. Some cemeteries allow the cremains of a family member to be placed in an occupied family plot or mausoleum If you wish to have the cremains placed in an occupied mausoleum or family plot, you need to call the cemetery and ask them to explain their policy as it relates to the burial of urns in occupied sites.

SCATTERED AT SEA

The decedent may have expressed a desire to have his ashes placed at sea. The funeral director or cremation director should be able to assist you in seeing to it that these wishes are respected. Federal law prohibits the ashes from being scattered any closer than three nautical miles from land, so you will need to arrange to have a boat carry the ashes out to sea (Title 40 of the Code of Federal Regulations ("CFR") Section 229.1).

If the decedent is to be buried in another state, then the body will need to be transported to that state. Most states, including New York, require a Transit Permit for burial or removal from the state where the death occurred (Pub. Health 4144). If services are to be held in New York and in another state, you can contact a local funeral director and he will make arrangements with the out-of-state funeral home for the transportation of the body.

If you do not plan to have services conducted in New York, you can contact the out-of-state funeral director and ask him to effect the transfer. Many funeral homes belong to a national network of funeral homes, so both the local and the out-of-state funeral director usually have the means to make arrangements to transport the body.

TRANSPORTING CREMAINS

If the body has been cremated, you can transport the cremains yourself, either by carrying the ashes as part of your carry-on luggage or by arranging with the airline to transport the ashes as cargo. Have a certified copy of the death certificate and the Transit Permit ready in the event that you need to identify the cremains of the decedent.

In these days of heightened security, it is important to call the airline before departure and ask whether they have any special regulation or procedure regarding the transportation of human ashes.

SPOUSE ► THE MILITARY BURIAL

Subject to availability of burial spaces, an honorably discharged veteran and his dependent child and his unremarried spouse may be buried in a national military cemetery. There are six national cemeteries in New York:

Bath National Cemetery   (607) 664-4853
Bath, NY

Calverton National Cemetery   (631) 727-5410
Calverton, NY

Cypress Hills National Cemetery   (631) 454-4949
Brooklyn, NY

Gerald B.H. Solomon Saratoga National Cemetery
Schuylerville, NY   (518) 581-9128

Long Island National Cemetery   (631) 454-4949
Farmingdale, NY

Woodlawn National Cemetery   (607) 664-4853
Elmira, NY

The Long Island and Woodlawn cemeteries are closed to new internments, however, they may have room for cremated remains or for the casketed remains of a family member of someone currently buried in that cemetery.

An honorably discharged veteran can also be buried in the national military cemetery at Arlington, Virginia. If you wish to have an eligible deceased veteran buried in the Arlington National Cemetery, call the Department of the Army at (703) 695-3250.

THE COST OF A MILITARY BURIAL

Burial space in a National Cemetery is free of charge. Cemetery employees will open and close the grave and mark it with a headstone or grave marker without cost to the family. If requested, the local Veteran's Administration ("VA") will provide the family with a memorial flag. The VA will not pay to have the body transported to the cemetery, so the family needs to make arrangements with a funeral firm to transport the remains to the cemetery.

Regardless of where an honorably discharged veteran is buried, allowances may be available for the plot, and the burial and grave marker expenses. The amount varies depending on factors such as whether the veteran died because of a service related injury. The VA will not reimburse any burial or funeral expense for the spouse of a veteran. For information about reimbursement of funeral and burial expenses you can call the VA at (800) 827-1000.

The Department of Veteran's Affairs has a Web site with information on the following topics:
- ➤ National and Military Cemeteries
- ➤ Burial, Headstones and Markers
- ➤ State Cemetery Grants Program
- ➤ Obtaining Military Records
- ➤ Locating Veterans

 VA CEMETERY WEB SITE
http://www.cem.va.gov

SPOUSE	BENEFITS FOR SPOUSE OF DECEASED VETERAN

The surviving spouse of an honorably discharged veteran should contact the Veteran's Administration to determine whether he/she is eligible for any benefits. For example, if the decedent had minor or disabled children, his spouse may also be eligible for a monthly benefit of Dependency and Indemnity Compensation ("DIC"). If the Veteran's surviving spouse receives nursing home care under Medicaid, the spouse might be eligible for monthly payments from the VA.

Whether a surviving spouse is eligible for any of these benefits depends on many factors including whether the decedent was serving on active duty, whether his death was service related, and the surviving spouse's assets and income. DIC benefits are discontinued should the surviving spouse re-marry; however, the law allows payments to be resumed in the event that the subsequent marriage ends because of death or divorce.

For information about whether the surviving spouse is eligible for any benefit related to the decedent's military service call the VA at (800) 827-1000. You can receive a printed statement of public policy: VA Pamphlet 051-000-00217-2 FEDERAL BENEFITS FOR VETERANS AND DEPENDENTS by sending a check in the amount of $5 to

THE SUPERINTENDENT OF DOCUMENTS
P.O. Box 371954
Pittsburgh, PA 15250-7954

Information is also available at the VA Web site.

 VETERAN'S ADMINISTRATION
http://www.va.gov

 **☎ LAWYER**   THE WRONGFUL DEATH

The decedent's family have the right to be compensated for any economic loss, including lost financial support, they suffer because of a ***wrongful death*** (a death caused by a wrongful act). Any family member can initiate a law suit, however, the defendant (or any other family member) can ask that the law suits be consolidated and pursued by the person appointed by the Court to settle the decedent's Estate. He can sue for the cost of medical bills and funeral expenses either for the decedent's Estate or to reimburse another who paid these expenses. Punitive damages may be awarded if the decedent could have received such an award had he lived (Est. Powers & Trusts 5-4.1, 5-4.3).

The Court will need to approved any proposed settlement. Whether the award is through trial or as a settlement, the case will need to be transferred to the Surrogate's Court for a hearing on the matter of how the funds should be divided and distributed (Est. Powers & Trusts 5-4.4, 5-4.6)

THE ACCIDENTAL DEATH
It is important to have a Personal Injury attorney investigate any accidental death, to determine whether the death was caused by the wrongful act of a person, or company. If the accident was related to the decedent's job, the family may wish to consult with a Worker's Compensation attorney as well.

VICTIMS OF CRIME
COMPENSATION PROGRAM

The NEW YORK STATE CRIME VICTIM BOARD provides financial assistance for crime victims and/or their families, who suffer losses that are not covered by insurance, public funds or any other compensation. Compensation can be awarded for burial expenses (up to $6,000), lost support up to $600 a week to a maximum of $30,000.

The Board will conduct a hearing to determine the amount of the award. The applicant has the right to be represented by an attorney before the Board. The Board can compensate up to $1,000 of those attorney's fees (Exec. 624, 626).

If the decedent died because of a criminal act, you may be eligible for assistance, provided the following is true:

➤ The decedent was an innocent victim.

➤ The crime was reported to authorities within a week of the discovery of the crime (Exec. 631).

➤ Application for compensation was filed within one year from the injury or death (Exec. 625).

To file a claim you can contact your local police department or District Attorney or your local Victim Service Agency (Exec. 625-a). The addresses and telephone numbers of Victim Service Agencies, and application forms are available at the Crime Victim Board Web site.

 NY STATE CRIME VICTIM BOARD
http://www.cvb.state.ny.us

The police will make every effort to identify and notify the family of an unclaimed body. Once notified the family has 24 hours to claim the body. If they are unable or unwilling to make burial arrangements, the person in charge of the body (hospital administrator, medical examiner, funeral director, etc.) will deliver the body to a New York medical school for the purpose of medical science and study (Pub. Health 4211).

If, before he died, the indigent or unidentified decedent asked that his body be buried, or if the decedent was carrying an identification card that indicated his opposition to the dissection or autopsy of his body, those wishes are respected, and the county will arrange for the burial (Pub. Health 4211 (3b)).

THE INDIGENT VETERAN
As explained previously, an honorably discharged veterans can be buried without charge — with the exception of transportation costs to the Veteran's cemetery.

DECEASED RECIPIENT OF PUBLIC ASSISTANCE
If a person, who was receiving Public Assistance (including Title XVI Social Security Income benefits) dies without funds to bury him, the Public Welfare official will require his spouse, or if he was under 21, his parent or stepparent, to pay for the burial. If the spouse or parent has insufficient monies to do so, the official will arrange for the burial (Social Services 101 and 141).

The funeral and burial industry is well regulated by both state and federal government. Under New York statute (Pub. Health 3450), the following acts are subject to disciplinary action:

☒ Delivering goods of a lesser quality than presented to the customer as a sample

☒ Using a false or misleading advertisement

☒ Paying kickbacks to generate business

☒ Being a habitual drunkard or addicted to drugs such as morphine, opium or cocaine.

Funeral directors are licensed professionals so it is unusual to have a problem with the funeral or burial or cremation. However, if you had a bad experience with any aspect of the funeral, you can call the state licensing agency at (518) 402-0785, or write to them:

Bureau of Funeral Directing
New York State Department of Health
Empire State Plaza, Corning Tower
Albany, NY 12237-0681

For burial or cemetery complaints, call the state consumer protection agency of the New York State Division of Cemeteries at (518) 474-6226. Or you can write to them: New York State Division of Cemeteries
162 Washington Avenue
Albany, NY 12231

In addition to filing a complaint with the Board, you may wish to consult with an attorney who is experienced in litigation matters to learn of any other legal remedy that you may have.

☎ LAWYER   THE MISSING BODY

Few things are more difficult to deal with than a missing person. The emotional turmoil created by the "not knowing" is often more difficult than the finality of death. The legal problems created by the disappearance are also more difficult than if the person simply died. It may take a two-part legal process — a Temporary Administration to handle the missing person's affairs while he is missing and then a final Probate proceeding if he is later declared dead or found dead:

APPOINTING A TEMPORARY ADMINISTRATOR

An *Absentee* is a missing person who cannot be found after a diligent search. If the Absentee has business matters that need attending (bills that need to be paid, checks that need to be cashed, etc.) someone, a *Temporary Administrator,* can be appointed by the Surrogate's Court to take charge of the missing person's property and manage it until he can be found (Surr. Ct. Proc. Act 901). You will need to employ an attorney who is experienced in Probate matters to get a Temporary Administrator appointed.

BEGINNING THE PROBATE PROCEDURE

The Temporary Administrator can begin Probate whenever the circumstances of the disappearance are sufficient to justify the belief that the missing person is dead or five years have passed, whichever is earlier. The Temporary Administrator can actually begin Probate after three years; however, should the Absentee appear before the five year period, he may have the right to reclaim his property, so it may be prudent to wait the five years (Est. Powers & Trusts 2-1.7, Surr. Ct. Proc. Act 911).

THE DEATH CERTIFICATE

It is the job of the funeral director to provide information about the decedent to the Registrar of Vital Statistics of the District where the death occurred (Pub. Health 4142). The New York State Department of Health is the agency in charge of filing death certificates for the state, with the exception of New York City. The New York City Department of Health and Mental Hygiene is the agency in charge of Vital Statistics for the city.

The Department in charge of Vital Statistics will prepare a death certificate base on information submitted by the funeral director. It is important that the information you give the funeral director is correct. You need to check the completed form to be sure names are correctly spelled and dates correctly written. Once the information is sent to the Department, it will be difficult and time consuming to make a correction.

The funeral director will order as many certified copies of the death certificate as you request. Most establishments require an original certified copy and not a photocopy so you need to order sufficient certified copies. The following is a list of institutions that may request a certified copy:

* Each insurance company that insured the decedent or his property (health, life, car, etc.)
* Each financial institution in which the decedent had money invested (brokerage houses, banks)
* The IRS
* The decedent's pension fund
* Each credit card company used by the decedent
* The Social Security Administration
* The Department of Motor Vehicles

Some airlines and car rental companies offer a discount for short notice, emergency trips. If you have family flying in for the funeral, you may wish to order a few extra copies of the death certificate so that they can obtain an airline or car rental discount. If you wish to order certified copies of the death certificate at a later date, you can call the funeral director and ask him to do so, or if you obtain a copy yourself.

Under New York law, death certificates are confidential records, so certified copies are limited to the spouse, child, parent or person appointed by the Court to settle the decedent's Estate. Anyone else requesting a death certificate will need to demonstrate to the Department that they have a lawful right or claim to the decedent's property.

The cost of obtaining a certified copy of the death certificate depends the agency issuing the document and the manner in which the order is placed. A New York City death certificate is $15.* A New York state certificate is $30.* There may be additional fees depending on how you place your order. Internet, fax and telephone requests must be paid by a major credit card. There is a vendor processing fee of $11.95* and a priority handling fee of $15.* *These are the rates as of January 2005.

TELEPHONE
You can call VitalCheck toll free at (877) 854-4481 to order a certified copy of the death certificate from New York City or New York State. They will give you information about current fees.

WALK-IN
Death Certificates are available from the local Registrar in the county where the death occurred (Pub. Health 4173).

BY MAIL

You can obtain a certified copy of the death certificate by writing to:

FOR NEW YORK STATE (not including New York City)
New York State Department of Health
Vital Records Section
Certification Unit
P.O. Box 2602
Albany, NY 12220-2602

FOR NEW YORK CITY

The New York State Department of Health does not issue death certificates for the City of New York. For deaths that occur within the city, write to:

NYC Department of Health and Mental Hygiene
Office of Vital Records
125 Worth Street, Box 4, Room 133
New York, NY 10013

VIA THE INTERNET

You can order the death certificate from the Web site of the N.Y. State Department of Health.

 N.Y. STATE DEPARTMENT OF HEALTH
http://www.health.state.ny.us

To order death certificates for those who died in New York City you will need to visit the New York City Department of Health and Mental Hygiene Web site.

 NYC DEPARTMENT OF HEALTH AND MENTAL HYGIENE
http://www.nyc.gov/health

About Probate

Once a person dies, all of the property he owns as of the date of his death is referred to as the **decedent's Estate.** If the decedent owned property that was in his name only (not jointly or in trust for someone), then some sort of court procedure may be necessary to determine who is entitled to ownership of the property. The name of the court procedure is **Probate**. We will use the term "Court" or "Probate Court" to refer to the judge who is presiding over Probate matters.

The root of the word Probate is "to prove." It refers to the first job of the Probate Court, that is, to examine proof of whether the decedent left a valid Will. The second job of the Probate Court is to appoint someone to wrap up the affairs of the decedent by paying the cost of the Probate procedure, any outstanding bills, and then distributing whatever is left to the proper beneficiary. If the decedent left a valid Will naming someone as *Executor* of his Estate, the Court will appoint that person for the job and issue *Letters Testamentary* giving him authority to administer the Estate. If he died without a Will, the Probate Court will appoint someone to be the *Administrator* of his Estate and issue *Letters of Administration.*

For simplicity we will refer to the person appointed by the court to settle the decedent's Estate as the **Personal Representative,** and the document authorizing him to act, as **Letters** (Est. Powers & Trusts 1-2.13).

There are different ways to conduct a Probate procedure depending on the value of the property that is being probated, and whether the decedent owned real property at the time of his death. We will refer to the property that is distributed as part of a Probate proceeding as the decedent's **Probate Estate** and the method of conducting the Probate, as the **Estate Administration**.

Chapter 6 explains the different kinds of Estate Administration that are available in the State of New York.

But we are getting ahead of ourselves. First, we need to determine whether a Probate procedure is necessary. To answer that question we need to know exactly what the decedent owned, so the next two chapters explain how to identify, and then locate, all of the decedent's assets.

Giving Notice Of The Death 2

Those closest to the decedent usually notify family members and close friends by telephone. The funeral director will arrange to have an obituary published in as many different newspapers as the family requests, but there is still the job of notifying the government and people who were doing business with the decedent. That job is the duty of whoever is appointed as Personal Representative of the decedent's Estate.

New York law gives an order of priority for the appointment of Personal Representative. Whoever the decedent named as Executor or Personal Representative of his Will has top priority. Once appointed, it is his job to give notice of the death.

If the decedent died *intestate*, i.e., without a valid Will, the surviving spouse has priority to be appointed as Personal Representative, so it is up to the spouse to let every one know of the death (Surr. Ct. Proc. Act 1001). If there is no spouse, the job falls to his next of kin. By *next of kin,* we mean those people who inherit the decedent's property according to New York's RULES GOVERNING INTESTATE SUCCESSION. Those laws are explained in Chapter 5.

The person who has the job of settling the decedent's Estate should begin to give notice as soon as is practicable after the death. Two government agencies that need to be notified are the Social Security Administration and the IRS. This chapter gives their telephone number as well as other agencies that need to be notified.

NOTIFYING SOCIAL SECURITY

Many funeral directors will, as part of their service package, notify the Social Security Administration of the death. You may wish to check to see that this has been done. You can do so by calling (800) 772-1213. If you are hearing impaired call (800) 325-0778 TTY. You will need to give the Social Security Administration the full legal name of the decedent as well as his Social Security number and date of birth.

> *Special Situation* | DECEDENT RECEIVING SOCIAL SECURITY
>
> If the decedent was receiving checks from Social Security, you need to determine whether his last check needs to be returned to the Social Security Administration. Each Social Security check is a payment for the prior month, provided that person lives for the entire prior month. If the decedent died on the last day of the month, you should not cash the check for that month.
>
> For example, if he died on July 31st, you need to return the check that the Social Security mailed out in August. If however, he died on August 1st the check sent in August need not be returned because that check was payment for the month of July.
>
> If the Social Security check is electronically deposited into a bank account, notify the bank and the Social Security Administration that the account holder died. If the check needs to be returned, the Social Security Administration will withdraw it electronically from the bank account. You will need to keep the account open until the funds are withdrawn.

SPOUSE → SPOUSE/CHILD'S SOCIAL SECURITY BENEFITS

If the decedent had sufficient work credits, the Social Security Administration will give the decedent's widow(er) or if unmarried, then the decedent's minor children, a one-time death benefit in the amount of $255.

SURVIVORS BENEFITS:

The spouse (or former spouse) of the decedent may be eligible for Survivors Benefits. Benefits vary depending on the amount of work credits earned by the decedent; whether the decedent had minor or disabled children; the spouse's age; how long they were married; etc. The minor child of the decedent may be eligible for benefits regardless of whether the child's father (the decedent) ever married the child's mother. Paternity can be established by any one of several methods including the father acknowledging his child in writing or verbally to members of his family. For more information you can call the Social Security Administration at (800) 772-1213.

SOCIAL SECURITY BENEFITS

A spouse or former spouse can collect social security benefits based on the decedent's work record. This value may be greater than the spouse now receives. It is important to make an appointment with your local Social Security office and determine whether you as the spouse (or former spouse) or parent of decedent's minor child are eligible for any Social Security or Survivor benefit. You can down load publications that explain survivors benefits from the Social Security Web site.

 SOCIAL SECURITY ADMINISTRATION
http://www.ssa.gov

DECEDENT WITH GOVERNMENT PENSION

Any pension or annuity check received after the date of death of a federal retiree, or a survivor annuitant, needs to be returned to the U.S. Treasury. If the check is direct deposited to a bank account, call the financial institution and ask them to return the check. If the check is sent by mail, you need to return it to the return mail address on the Department of Treasury envelope in which the check was mailed. Include a letter explaining the reason for the return of the check and stating the decedent's date of death.

$$$ APPLY FOR BENEFITS $$$

A survivor annuity may be available to a surviving spouse, and/or minor or disabled child. In some cases, a former spouse may be eligible for benefits. Even though you notify the government of the death, they will not automatically give you benefits to which you may be entitled. You need to apply for those benefits by notifying the Office of Personnel Management ("OPM") of the death and requesting that they send you an application for survivor benefits. You can call them at (888) 767-6738 or you can write to:

U. S. OFFICE OF PERSONNEL MANAGEMENT
RETIREMENT OPERATIONS CENTER
Post Office Box 45
Boyers, PA 16017-4500

You will find brochures and information about Survivor's Benefits at the OPM Web site.

 U.S. OFFICE OF PERSONNEL MANAGEMENT
http://www.opm.gov

Special *Situation*	DECEDENT WITH COMPANY PENSION OR ANNUITY

In most cases, pension and annuity checks are payment for the prior month. If the decedent received his pension or annuity check before his death, then no monies need be returned. Pension checks and/or annuity checks received after the date of death may need to be returned to the company. You need to notify the company of the death to determine the status of the last check sent to the decedent.

Before notifying the company, locate the policy or pension statement that is the basis of the income. That document should tell whether there is a beneficiary of the pension or annuity funds now that the pensioner or annuitant is dead. If you cannot locate the document, use the return address on the check envelope and ask the company to send you a copy of the plan. Also request that they forward to you any claim form that may be required in order for the survivor or beneficiary to receive benefits under that pension plan or policy.

If the pension/annuity check is direct deposited to the decedent's account, then ask the bank to assist you in locating the company and notifying the company of the death.

Anyone who is a beneficiary of an Individual Retirement Account ("IRA") or QRP needs to keep in mind that income taxes may not have been paid on monies placed in an IRA or QRP account. In such case, significant taxes may be due when the money is withdrawn. You need to learn what options are available to you as a beneficiary of the plan and the tax consequences of each option. You will need to ask an accountant how much will be due in taxes for each option. Once you know all the facts, you will be able to make the best choice for your circumstance.

There are special options available if the spouse is the beneficiary of the decedent's IRA account. The spouse has the right to withdraw the money from the account or roll it over into the spouse's own retirement account. Although the employer can explain options that are available, the spouse still needs to understand the tax consequence of choosing any given option. It is important to consult with an accountant to determine the best way to go.

If the decedent had a QRP, the plan may permit the spouse to roll the balance of the account into a new IRA. The spouse needs to contact the decedent's employer for an explanation of the plan and all the options that are available at this time.

NOTIFYING IRS

THE FINAL INCOME TAX RETURN

The surviving spouse can file a final joint income tax return. If there is no surviving spouse, it becomes the of the Personal Representative to do so. If Probate is not necessary, whoever takes possession of the decedent's property needs to file his final return.

Monies earned within the state of New York are subject to a state income tax, and that tax is imposed regardless of whether the decedent was a resident of New York. The decedent's final federal income tax return (IRS form 1040) needs to be filed by April 15th of the year following the year in which he died. The state income tax is filed at the same time (Tax Law 651). You can get information about filing the final New York return by calling the Income Tax Division of the Department of Taxation and Finance at (800) 225-5829, or you can visit their Web site.

 NY STATE DEPT. OF TAXATION AND FINANCE
http://www.tax.state.ny.us

You may want to keep the decedent's bank account open until you determine whether the decedent is entitled to an income tax refund. See Chapter 6 for an explanation of how to obtain a tax refund.

THE GOOD NEWS

Monies inherited from the decedent are generally not counted as income to you, so you do not pay federal income tax on those monies. If the monies you inherit later earn interest or income for you, then of course you will report that income as you do any other type of income.

Both the federal and state government have the right to impose an **Estate Tax** on property transferred to a beneficiary as a result of the death. All the property owned as of the date of death becomes the decedent's **Taxable Estate.** This includes *real property* (residential lots, condominiums etc.) and *personal property* (life insurance policies, cars, business interests, securities, IRA accounts, etc.). It includes property held in the decedent's name alone, as well as property that he held jointly or in Trust. It also includes gifts given by the decedent during his lifetime that exceeded $10,000 per person, per year. In the year 2002, the **Annual Gift Tax Exclusion** was adjusted for inflation to $11,000 (26 U.S.C 2503).

For most of us, this is not a concern because no federal Estate Tax need be paid unless the decedent's Taxable Estate exceeds the federal **Estate Tax Exclusion** amount. That value is currently one and a half million dollars and is scheduled to go even higher:

YEAR	ESTATE TAX EXCLUSION AMOUNT
2004-2005	$1,500,000
2006-2008	$2,000,000
2009	$3,500,000

Under current law, the federal Estate Tax is scheduled to be phased out in the year 2010, but reinstated once again in the year 2011 with an Exclusion Amount of $1,000,000 — unless lawmakers change the tax law once again.

There is an unlimited marital tax deduction for property transferred to the surviving spouse who is a U.S. citizen; so in most cases, no Estate tax need be paid if the decedent was married. Regardless of whether taxes are due, federal and state Estate tax returns must be filed whenever the decedent's Estate exceeds the federal Estate Tax Exclusion Amount in effect as of his date of death. Both state and federal returns are due within 9 months of the date of death.

THE NEW YORK ESTATE TAX

Although the federal government does not impose an Estate Tax for Estates for over the Exclusion Amount, the state of New York imposes an Estate Tax on those Taxable Estates in excess of $1,000,000 (Tax Law 951). For example, in the year 2006, a Taxable Estate of $3,000,000 will pay an Estate Tax to the state of New York on anything over $1,000,000 and a federal Estate Tax on anything over $2,000,000 — provided the tax law does not change still again before that time.

The New York Estate Tax applies to all of the property owned by a deceased resident of the state, as well as property transferred within the state because of the death of a non-resident of the state.

Both state and federal government do not tax property passing to the decedent's spouse, however, once the surviving spouse dies, all of his Estate is subject to Estate Taxes. As we will see in Chapter 7, setting up a Revocable Living Trust can significantly reduce the amount of Estate Taxes that may need to be paid once the surviving spouse dies.

THE UN-UNIFIED GIFT TAX

Up until the year 2002, if you gave someone more than $10,000 in any given year you had to report that gift to the IRS. As explained, the Annual Gift Tax Exclusion is now adjusted for the cost of living and is currently $11,000. The IRS keeps a running count of amounts you give to someone that exceed the Annual Gift Tax Exclusion. Although you are required to report amounts over the Annual Exclusion value, no tax is due unless that running total is more than the federal lifetime Gift Tax Exclusion amount. If your running total does not exceed that amount during your lifetime, once you die, the cumulative value of gifts reported to the IRS will be added to your Taxable Estate.

Up until the change in the tax law in 2001, the Gift and Estate Tax were unified. No Gift Tax needed to be paid unless the total value of the taxable gifts exceeded the federal Estate Tax Exclusion amount. That changed in 2004. In 2004, the federal Estate Tax Exclusion amount went up to $1,500,000, but the amount for the Gift Tax Exclusion remained at $1,000,000, so they are no longer unified.

To summarize:
If you make a gift to someone that is greater than the Annual Gift Tax Exclusion for that year, you must report the gift to the IRS. The IRS will keep count of values that you gave in excess of the Annual Gift Tax Exclusion. In 2004, and thereafter, if that sum exceeds $1,000,000, you will pay a Gift Tax on any amount you give that is over the Annual Gift Tax Exclusion. The Estate Tax is scheduled to be repealed in 2010, but not the Gift Tax.

New York does not have a Gift Tax at this time.

The current federal Estate tax is scheduled to be phased out in the year 2010, but a new Capital Gains Tax is scheduled for 2010 that may prove even more costly than the Estate Tax. The new Capital Gains Tax is related to the way inherited property is evaluated by the federal government. Real and personal property is inherited at a "step up" in basis, meaning that if the decedent's property has increased in value from the time he acquired it, the beneficiary will inherit the property at its fair market value as of the decedent's date of death. For example, if the decedent bought stock for $20,000 and it is worth $50,000 as of his date of death, there is a $30,000 step-up in basis, i.e., the beneficiary inherits the stock at the current $50,000 value. If the beneficiary sells the stock for $50,000, he pays no Capital Gains Tax. If the beneficiary holds onto the stock and later sells it for $60,000, the beneficiary will pay a Capital Gains Tax only on the $10,000 increase in value since the decedent's death.

Up to 2009, there is no limit to the amount a beneficiary can take as a step-up in basis. But in 2010 caps are set in place. The decedent's Estate will be allowed a 1.3 million dollar step-up in basis, plus another 3 million for property passing to the surviving spouse. The new law could result in significant Capital Gains Taxes that the beneficiary must pay. For example, suppose in 2010 you inherit a business from your father that he purchased for $100,000 and it is now worth 2 million dollars. There is a capital gain of 1.9 million dollars, but you are allowed a step-up in basis of only 1.3 million. If you sell it for 2 million dollars, $600,000 of your inheritance will be subject to a Capital Gains Tax.

SPOUSE ➤ SELLING THE HOME

In the tough "ole days" the IRS used to allow Capital Gains Tax Exclusion (up to $125,000) on the sale of one's *homestead* (the principal residence). A person had to be 55 or older to take advantage of the Exclusion, and it was a once-in-a-lifetime tax break. If a married couple sold their home and took the Tax Exclusion it was "used up" and no longer available to either partner.

In these, the good times, the IRS allows you to sell your home and up to $250,000 ($500,000 for a married couple) is excluded from the Capital Gains Tax. There is no limit to the number of times you can use the Exclusion, provided you own and live in the home at least two of the last five years prior to the sale (26 U.S.C. 121).

If, under the old law, the decedent and his spouse used their "once in a lifetime" Homestead Tax Exclusion, with this new law, the surviving spouse can sell the homestead and once again take advantage of a tax break.

Special Situation	BENEFICIARY OF THE NEW YORK HOME

People who own and occupy a residence in New York are entitled to a School Tax Relief Exemption ("STAR"). The exempt amount is determined annually (Real Prop. Tax 425). In addition to STAR, persons of low income who are 65 or older and/or have a disability are entitled to have a certain percentage of their assessed valuation exempt from property taxes (Real Prop. Tax 467, 459, 459-c).

If the new owner is going to occupy the property as his home, he needs to apply to the county Assessor's Office for his own tax exemption. The Assessor must be notified of the change of ownership, regardless of whether the new owner intends to occupy the property as his primary residence.

You can get information about property tax exemptions by calling the Office of Real Property Services at (518) 486-5446, or you can visit their Web site for property tax information and the location of the nearest county Assessor.

 OFFICE OF REAL PROPERTY SERVICES
http://www.orps.state.ny.us

A decedent who was the **Grantor** (or *Settlor*) of a Trust, was probably managing the Trust as *Trustee* during his lifetime. The document that sets out the terms of the Trust (the **Trust Agreement)** should name a **Successor Trustee** to manage the Trust now that the Grantor is deceased. The Agreement may instruct the Successor Trustee to make certain gifts once the Grantor dies or the Trust document may direct the Successor Trustee to hold money in trust for a beneficiary of the Trust.

IF YOU ARE SUCCESSOR TRUSTEE

If you are the Successor Trustee, then in addition to following the terms of the Trust, you are required to obey all of the laws of the state of New York relating to the administration of the Trust. You should consult with an attorney experienced in Estate Planning to help you administer the Trust according to the law and without any liability to yourself.

IF YOU ARE A BENEFICIARY OF THE TRUST

If you are a beneficiary of the Trust, you need to obtain a copy of the Trust to learn how the Trust will be administered now that the Grantor or Settlor is deceased. Most Trust documents are written in "legalese," so you may want to employ your own attorney to review the Trust and explain to you what rights you have under the Trust.

People and companies who were doing business with the decedent need to be notified of his death. This includes utility companies, credit card companies, banks, brokerage firms and any company that insured the decedent.

NOTIFY CREDIT CARD COMPANIES

You need to notify the decedent's credit card companies of the death. If you can find the contract with the credit card company, check to see whether the decedent had credit card insurance. If the decedent had credit card insurance, then the balance of the account is now paid in full. If you cannot find the contract, contact the company and get a copy of the contract along with a statement of the balance due as of the date of death.

DESTROY DECEDENT'S CREDIT CARDS

You need to destroy all of the decedent's credit cards. If you hold a credit card jointly with the decedent, then it is important to waste no time in closing that account and opening another in your name only.

That's something Barbara knows from hard experience. She and Hank never married but they did live together for several years before he died from liver disease. Hank came from a well to do family so he had enough money to support himself and Barbara during his long illness. Hank put Barbara on all of his credit card accounts so that she could purchase things when he became too ill to go shopping with her. After the funeral, Barbara had a gathering of friends and family at their apartment. Barbara was so preoccupied with her loss that she never noticed that Hank's credit cards were missing until the bills started coming in.

Barbara did not know who ran up the bills on Hank's credit cards during the month following his death. It was obvious that Hank's signature had been forged — but who forged it? One credit card company suspected that it might have been Barbara herself to get out of paying the bill by saying that the card had been stolen

Because the cards were held jointly, Barbara became liable to either pay the charges to the credit card or prove that she did not make the purchases. She was able to clear her credit record but it took several months and she had to employ an attorney to help her do so.

NOTIFY INSURANCE COMPANIES

Examine the decedent's financial records to determine the name and telephone number of all of the companies that insured the decedent or his property. This includes real property insurance, motor vehicle insurance, health insurance and life insurance.

MOTOR VEHICLE INSURANCE
Locate the insurance policy for any type of motor vehicle owed by the decedent (car, truck, boat, airplane) and notify the insurance company of the death. Determine how long insurance coverage continues after the death. Ask the insurance agent to explain what things are covered under the policy. Is the motor vehicle covered for all types of casualty (theft, accident, vandalism, etc.) or is coverage limited in some way?

If you can continue coverage, then determine when the next insurance payment is due. Hopefully, the car will be sold or transferred to a beneficiary before that date, but if not, you need to arrange for sufficient insurance coverage during the Probate procedure.

Special Situation ▷ ACCIDENTAL DEATH

If the decedent died as a result of an accident, then check for all possible sources of accident insurance coverage including his homeowner's policy. Some credit card companies provide accident insurance as part of their contract with their card holders. If the decedent died in an automobile accident, check to see whether he was covered by any type of travel insurance, such as rental car insurance. If he belonged to an automobile club, such as AAA, check whether he had accident insurance as part of his club membership.

LIFE INSURANCE COMPANIES

If the decedent's life was insured, you need to locate the policy and notify the company of his death. Call each life insurance company and ask what they require in order to forward the insurance proceeds to the beneficiary. Most companies will ask you to send them the original policy and a certified copy of the death certificate. Send the original policy by certified mail or any of the overnight services that require a signed receipt for the package. Make a copy of the original policy for your records before mailing the original policy to the company.

BANK ACCOUNT LIFE INSURANCE

Many banks, credit unions, savings and loan associations provide life insurance at no cost to the primary owner of the account. While the amounts are generally small ($1,000 to $5,000), it is insurance that is often overlooked when settling the decedent's affairs. If you do not find a record of such policy, contact each financial institution to determine whether such insurance is provided by the company.

IF YOU CANNOT LOCATE THE POLICY

If you know that the decedent was insured, but you cannot locate the insurance policy, you can contact the company and request a copy of the policy. A tougher question is how to locate the policy if you do not know the name of the insurance company. The American Council of Life Insurers offers suggestions that you may find helpful at the Missing Policy Inquiry page of their Web site.

 AMERICAN COUNCIL OF LIFE INSURERS
http://www.acli.com

IF YOU CANNOT LOCATE THE COMPANY

If you cannot locate the insurance company it may be doing business under another name or it may no longer be doing business in the state of New York. Each state has a branch of government that regulates insurance companies doing business in that state. If you are having difficulty locating the insurance company you can call the Department of Insurance in the state where the policy was purchased and ask for assistance in locating the company. In New York you can call the Department of Insurance at (212-480-6400). In state you can call (800) 342-3736; or you can visit the INSURANCE COMPANY SEARCH section of their Web site.

 NEW YORK STATE INSURANCE DEPARTMENT
http://www.ins.state.ny.us

EAGLE PUBLISHING COMPANY OF BOCA has the telephone number of the Insurance Department for each state at the PUBLIC INFORMATION section on its Web site.
http://www.eaglepublishing.com

WORK RELATED INSURANCE

If the decedent was employed, check his records for information about work related benefits. He may have survivor benefits from a company or group life insurance plan and/or a retirement plan. Also check with the employer to see whether there are company benefits. If the decedent belonged to a union, ask whether there are any union benefits.

The decedent may have belonged to a professional, fraternal or social organization such as the local Chamber of Commerce, a Veteran's organization, the Kiwanis, AARP, the Rotary Club, etc. If he belonged to any such organization check to see whether the organization provided any type of insurance coverage.

 BUSINESS OWNED BY DECEDENT

If the decedent owned his own company or was a partner in a company, he may have purchased "key man" insurance. Key man insurance is a policy designed to protect the company should a valuable employee become disabled or die. Benefits are paid to the company to compensate the company for the loss of someone who is essential to the continuation of the business. Ultimately the policy benefits those who inherit the business.

If the decedent had an ownership interest in an ongoing business (sole proprietor, shareholder or partner), there may be a shareholder's or partnership agreement requiring the company to purchase the decedent's share of the business. The Personal Representative or his attorney needs to investigate to see if there was a key man insurance policy and/or such purchase agreement.

If the decedent was the sole owner of a corporation and the company stock was in his name only, there may need to be a Probate proceeding before the company can be transferred to the new owner.

The New York Secretary of State serves as the Registered Agent for every corporation within the state. In addition, a company may appoint someone to serve as their Registered Agent (Bus. Corp. 305). If the decedent was the sole officer and/or Registered Agent of the company, the Division of Corporations needs to be notified of the identity of the new officers and Registered Agent as soon as is practicable. Forms to change officers and/or Registered Agent can be obtained by writing to:

NY State Department of State
Division of Corporations, State Record
41 State Street
Albany, NY 12231-0001

or you can download the form from the Corporations and Business Entities section of the New York Department of State Web site.

 New York Department of State
http://www.dos.state.ny.us

If you were not actively involved in running the business, you might want to call the Corporations Division at (518) 474-1418 for information about the company (names, addresses of officers and directors, number of company shares, whether fees are current, etc.). You can also obtain this information at the above Web site.

HOMEOWNER'S INSURANCE

If the decedent owned his own home, then check whether there is sufficient insurance coverage on the property. The decedent may have neglected to increase his insurance as the property appreciated in value. If you think the property may be vacant for some period of time, then it is important to have vandalism coverage included in the policy. Once the property is sold, or transferred to the proper beneficiary, you can have the policy discontinued or transferred to the new owner. The decedent's Estate should receive a refund for the unused portion of the premium.

MORTGAGE INSURANCE
If the decedent had a mortgage on any parcel of real estate that he owned, he might have arranged with his lender for an insurance policy that pays off the mortgage balance in the event of his death. Look at the closing statement to see whether there was a charge for mortgage insurance. Also check with the lender to determine if such a policy was purchased.

If there was no mortgage insurance, and the decedent was the sole owner, the beneficiary of the property needs to make arrangements with the lender to continue making payments on the mortgage or to refinance the loan.

NOTIFY THE HOMEOWNER'S ASSOCIATION
If the decedent owned a condominium or a residence regulated by a homeowner's association, the association needs to be notified of the change of ownership. Once the property is transferred, the new owner will need to contact the association to learn of the rules and regulations of the association. The new owner will need to arrange to have notices of dues and assessments forwarded to him.

HEALTH INSURANCE

The Health Insurance carrier probably knows of the death, but it is a good idea to contact them to determine what coverage the decedent had under that insurance plan. If you cannot find the original policy, have the insurance company send you a copy of the policy so that you can determine whether medical treatment given to the decedent before his death was covered by that policy.

 **DECEDENT ON MEDICARE**

If the decedent was covered by Medicare, you do not need to notify anyone, but you do need to know what things were covered by Medicare so that you can determine what medical bills are (or are not) covered by Medicare. The government publication **MEDICARE AND YOU** (Publication No. CMS-10050) explains what things are covered under Medicare and the different kinds of plans that are currently available. You can get the publication by writing to:

U.S. Dept. of Health and Human Services
Centers for Medicare and Medicaid Services
7500 Security Boulevard
Baltimore, MD 21244-1850

You can download the publication from the Internet.

 MEDICARE WEB SITE
http://www.medicare.gov

The publication is available on Audiotape, in Braille, in large print and in Spanish. To receive a copy you can call (800) 633-4227. TTY users call (877) 486-2048.

SPOUSE — THE SPOUSE'S HEALTH INSURANCE

If the spouse of the decedent is insured under Medicare, then the death does not affect the surviving spouse's coverage. If the spouse was not covered by Medicare but has her own health insurance that also covered the decedent, then the spouse needs to notify the employer of the death because this may affect the cost of the plan to the employer and/or the spouse. If the spouse was covered under the decedent's policy, he/she needs to arrange for new coverage. There are state and federal laws that ensure continued coverage under the decedent's policy for a period of time depending on whether the decedent's employer falls under federal or state regulation.

If the decedent was employed by a federally regulated company (usually a company with at least twenty employees), under the Consolidated Omnibus Budget Reconciliation Act ("COBRA") the employer must make the company health plan available to the surviving spouse and any dependent child of the decedent for at least 36 months. The employer is required to give notice to the surviving spouse that the spouse and/or dependent child have the right to continue coverage under the decedent's health plan. The spouse and/or child have 60 days from the date of death or 60 days after the employer sends notice (whichever is later) to tell the employer whether the surviving spouse and child wish to continue with the health insurance plan (29 U.S.C. Sec. 1162, 1163, 1165). The only problem with continued coverage may be the cost. Before the death, the employer may have been paying some percentage of the premium. The employer has no such duty after the death unless there was some employment agreement stating otherwise.

Under COBRA, the employer may charge the spouse for the full cost of the plan plus a 2% administrative fee. If you have a question about your coverage under COBRA, you can call the U.S. Department of Labor ("DOL") at (800) 998-7542 and ask for the number of your local DOL office. You can also ask that they send you their publication HEALTH BENEFITS UNDER COBRA; or you can visit their Web site for more information.

 U.S. DEPARTMENT OF LABOR
http://www.dol.gov/

HEALTH INSURANCE COVERAGE UNDER NEW YORK LAW
Under New York law, health insurance policies must contain a provision that coverage will continue for surviving spouse and dependent children of a deceased policy holder (Ins. 3221).

The decedent's employer should promptly notify the surviving spouse about options that are available for continued coverage under the decedent's existing group health insurance plan. If you do not receive notice within two weeks of the death, you should call (and write) to the employer requesting such information. If notice is not promptly received or the employer reports that you are not eligible for continued coverage, check with the New York State Insurance Department for information about your rights under state law. You can call them at (212) 480-5242. In state, call (800) 342-3736.

You can also find health insurance information by visiting their Web site.   http://www.ins.state.ny.us

NOTIFY ADVERTISERS

Probably the last in the world to learn of the decedent's death is the direct mail advertiser. Advertisers are nothing if not tenacious. It is not uncommon for advertisements to be mailed to the decedent for more than ten years after the death. It is not because the advertiser is trying to sell something to the decedent, but rather the people who prepare (and sell) mailing lists do not know that he is dead.

Those who sell mailing lists may not be motivated to update the list because of the cost of doing the necessary research; and perhaps because the price of the mailing list is often based on the number of people on the list. Even those who compose their own list may decide it is less costly to mail to everyone, than take the time (and money) to update the list.

If it gives you pleasure to think of advertisers spending substantial sums for nothing, then that is what you should do (nothing). But for those of you who wince each time you see another piece of mail addressed to the decedent, you can write to the Direct Marketing Association and ask that the name be deleted from all mailing lists:

Mail Preference Service
Direct Marketing Association
P.O. Box 9008
Farmingdale, NY 11735

You will need to give them the decedent's complete address, including zip code and every name variation that the decedent may have used; for example:

Theodore James Jones
Ted Jones   Ted J. Jones
T. J. Jones   T. James Jones
Jim Jones, etc.

CHANGE BENEFICIARIES

If the decedent was someone you named as beneficiary of your insurance policy, Will, Trust, brokerage account or pension plan, then you may need to name another beneficiary in his place:

INSURANCE POLICY

If you named the decedent as the primary beneficiary of your life insurance policy, check to see whether you named a contingent (alternate) beneficiary in the event that the decedent did not survive you. If not, you need to contact the insurance company and name a new beneficiary. If you did name a contingent beneficiary, that person is now your primary beneficiary and you need to consider whether you wish to name a new contingent beneficiary at this time.

HEALTH INSURANCE POLICY

If the decedent was covered under your health insurance policy, your employer and the health insurer need to be notified of the death because this may affect the cost of the plan to you and/or your employer.

WILL OR TRUST

Most Wills provide for a contingent beneficiary in the event that the person named as beneficiary dies first. If you named the decedent as your beneficiary, check to see whether you named an alternate beneficiary. If not, you need to have your attorney revise your Will and name a new beneficiary.

Similarly, if you are the Grantor or Settlor of a Trust and the decedent was one of the beneficiaries of your Trust, check the Trust document to see if you named an alternate beneficiary. If not, contact your attorney to prepare an amendment to the Trust, naming a new beneficiary.

BANK AND SECURITIES ACCOUNTS ✍

If the decedent was a beneficiary or joint owner of your bank or securities account, you may wish to arrange for a new beneficiary or joint owner at this time.

PENSION PLANS ✍

If the decedent was a beneficiary under your pension plan, you need to notify them of his death and name a new beneficiary. Many pension plans require that you notify them within a set period of time (usually 30 days) so it is important to notify them as soon as you are able. If the decedent was a beneficiary of your Individual Retirement Account ("IRA") or of your Qualified Retirement Plan ("QRP") and you did not provide for an alternate beneficiary, you need to name another beneficiary.

Before you choose an alternate beneficiary, it is important that you understand all of the options available to you. Not an easy task. There are many complex government regulations relating to IRA and QRP accounts. Even if you believe you understood your options when you set up your account, the federal government often changes those options.

Your choice of beneficiary might impact the amount of money you can withdraw each month, so it is important to consult with your accountant, tax attorney or financial planner, before you make your election.

NOTIFYING CREDITORS

It is the job of the person appointed as Personal Representative to notify the decedent's creditors of the death so that the creditor is given an opportunity to come forward and file a *claim* (a written demand for payment) for monies owed. The attorney for the Personal Representative usually takes care of the notice procedure. We will explain that procedure later in this book.

If no Probate proceeding is necessary, the next of kin can notify the creditors of the death, but before doing so, it is important to read Chapter 4: **WHAT BILLS NEED TO BE PAID?** That chapter explains what bills need to be paid and who is responsible to pay them.

Before any bill can be paid, you need to know whether the decedent left any asset that can be used to pay those debts. The next chapter explains how to identify, and then locate all of the property owned by the decedent.

Locating the Assets 3

It is important to locate the financial records of the decedent and then carefully examine those records. Even the partner of a long-term marriage should conduct a thorough search because the surviving spouse may be unaware of all that was owned (or owed) by the decedent.

It is not unusual for a surviving spouse to be surprised when learning of the decedent's business transactions, especially in those cases where the decedent had control of family finances. One such example is that of Sam and Henrietta. They married just as soon as Sam was discharged from the army after World War II. During their marriage, Sam handled all of the finances giving Henrietta just enough money to run the household.

Every now and again Henrietta would think of getting a job. She longed to have her own source of income and some economic independence. Each time she brought up the subject Sam would loudly object. He had no patience for this new "woman's lib" thing. Sam said he got married to have a real wife — one who would cook his meals and keep house for him.

Henrietta was not the arguing type. She rationalized, saying that Sam had a delicate stomach and dust allergies. He needed her to prepare his special meals and keep an immaculate house for him. Besides, Sam had a good job with a major cruise line and he needed her to accompany him on his frequent business trips.

Once Sam retired, he was even more cautious in his spending habits. Henrietta seldom complained. She assumed the reason for his "thrift" was that they had little money and had to live on his pension.

They were married 52 years when Sam died at the age of 83. Henrietta was 81 at the time of his death. She was one very happy, very angry and very aged widow when she discovered that Sam left her with assets worth well over a million dollars!

LOCATING RECORDS

As you go through the papers of the decedent you may come across documents that indicate property ownership, such as bank registers, stock or bond certificates, insurance policies, pension or annuity records, etc. Place all evidence of ownership in a single place. You will need to contact the different companies in order to transfer title to the proper beneficiary.

To obtain the property, you may need to produce evidence of the decedent's personal relationships, such as a marriage or birth certificate, or naturalization papers, or military personnel records. If you cannot locate the decedent's marriage or birth certificate, you can get a copy of those records from the Vital Records office in the state where the event took place. Many states (including New York) restrict access to these records to close family members or to the decedent's Personal Representative. See chapter 1 for the telephone number of New York's Vital Record's office. You can find the location and telephone number of the Vital Records of other states by calling information or you can use the Internet to locate the office by using your favorite search engine to find Vital Statistics or Vital Records.

You can obtain a copy of the military record of a deceased veteran by writing to:

The National Personnel Records Center
Military Personnel Records
9700 Page Avenue
St. Louis, MO   63132-5100

They will send you form SF 180 to complete. You can get the form from the Internet at http://www.cem.va.gov or from the National Archives and Records Administration Fax-On-Demand system. Dial (301) 713-6905 and request document number 2255.

COLLECT AND IDENTIFY KEYS

The decedent may have kept his records in a safe deposit box, so you may find that your first job is to locate the keys to the box. As you go through the personal effects of the decedent, collect and identify all the keys that you find. If you come across an unidentified key, it could be a key to a post office box (private or federal) or a safe deposit box located in a bank or in a private vault company. You will need to determine whether that key opens a box that contains property belonging to the decedent or whether the key is to a box no longer in use. Some ways to investigate are as follows:

☑ CHECK BUSINESS RECORDS

If the decedent kept receipts, look through those items to see if he paid for the rental of a post office or safe deposit box. Also, look at his check register to see if he wrote a check to the Postmaster or to any safe deposit or vault company. Look at his bank records to see if there is any bank charge for a safe deposit box. Some banks bill separately for safe deposit boxes so check with all of the banks in which the decedent had an account to determine if he had a safe deposit box with that bank.

☑ CHECK THE KEY TYPE

If you cannot identify the key, then take it to each local locksmith and ask whether anyone can identify the type of facility that uses such keys. If that doesn't work, go to each bank, post office and private safe deposit box company where the decedent shopped, worked or frequented and ask whether they use the type of key that you found.

☑ CHECK THE MAIL

Check the mail over the next several months to see if the decedent receives a statement requesting payment for the next year's rental of a post office or safe deposit box.

You may find evidence of a brokerage account, bank account, or safe deposit box by examining correspondence addressed to the decedent. If the decedent was living alone, have his mail forwarded to the person he named as Personal Representative or Executor of his Will. If the decedent did not leave a Will, and no Probate procedure is necessary, the mail should be forwarded to his next of kin. Call the Postmaster and ask him/her to send you the necessary forms to make the change. Request that the mail be forwarded for the longest period allowed by law (currently one year).

The decedent may have been renting a post office box at his local post office branch or perhaps at the branch closest to where he did his banking. Ask the Postmaster to help you determine whether the decedent was renting a post office box. If so, then you need to locate the key to the box so that you can collect the decedent's mail.

 LOST POST OFFICE BOX KEY

If the decedent had a post office box and you cannot locate it, contact the local postmaster and ask him what documentation is needed for you to get possession of the mail in that box. As before, you will ask the Post-master to have all future mail addressed to that box , forwarded to the Personal Representative, or if no Probate is necessary, to the decedent's next of kin.

WHAT TO DO WITH CHECKS

You may receive checks in the mail made out to the decedent. Social Security checks, pension checks and annuity checks issued after the date of death may need to be returned to the sender. (See pages 30 and 32 of this book.) Other checks need to be deposited. If Probate is necessary, the Personal Representative will open a Probate Estate account and will deposit the decedent's checks to that account.

If Probate is not necessary, checks can be deposited to any account held in the name of the decedent. The decedent is not here to endorse the check, but you can deposit it to his account by writing his bank account number on the back of the check and printing beneath it **FOR DEPOSIT ONLY.**

The bank will accept such an endorsement and deposit the check into the decedent's account. If the check is significant in value or the decedent had different accounts that are accessible to different people, then there needs to be cooperation and a sense of fair play. If not, the dollar gain may not nearly offset the emotional turmoil.

Such was the case with Gail. Her father made her a joint owner of his checking account to assist in paying his bills. He had macular degeneration and it was increasingly difficult for him to see. The father also had a savings account that was in his name only.

Gail's brother Ken had a good paying job in Alaska. Even though he lived at a distance, Ken, his wife and two children always spent the Christmas holidays with his father and sister.

Each summer, their father enjoyed leaving the heat of New York to spend a few weeks in the cool Alaskan climate.

One summer, the father purchased a round trip ticket to Alaska. It cost several hundred dollars. Just before the departure date, the father had a heart attack and died. Gail called the airline to cancel the ticket. They refunded the money in a check made out to her father. She deposited the check to the joint account, and then closed it out.

As part of the Probate procedure, the money in the father's savings account was divided equally between Ken and his sister. Ken wondered what happened to the money from the airline tickets.

Gail explained "Dad paid for the tickets from the joint account, so I deposited the money back to that account. "

"Aren't you going to give me half?"

"Dad meant for me to have whatever was in that joint account. If he wanted you to have half of the money, he would have made you joint owner as well."

Ken didn't see it that way "That refund was part of Dad's Estate. It should have been deposited to his savings account to be divided equally between us. Are you going to force me to argue this in Court?"

Gail finally agreed to split the money with Ken, but the damage was done.

Gail complains that holidays are lonely since Dad died.

LOCATE FINANCIAL RECORDS

To locate the decedent's assets you need to find evidence of what he owned and where those assets are located. His financial records should lead you to the location of all of his assets, so your first job is to locate those records. The best place to start the search is in the decedent's home. Many people keep their financial records in a single place but it is important to check the entire house to be sure you did not miss something.

CHECK THE COMPUTER

Don't overlook that computer sitting silently in the corner. It may hold the decedent's check register and all of his financial records. You may want to monitor his e-mail for e-bank or on-line credit card accounts.

The computer may be programmed to protect this information. If you cannot access the decedent's financial records, you may need to employ a computer technician or computer consultant who will be able to print out all of the information on the hard drive of the computer. You can find such a technician or consultant by looking in the telephone book under COMPUTER SUPPORT SERVICES or COMPUTER SYSTEM DESIGNS & CONSULTANTS.

LOCATE TITLE TO MOTOR VEHICLE

The New York State Department of Motor Vehicles is in charge of the title and registration of motor vehicles, including motorized scooters and bicycles and boats that are 14" in length or greater. The Department also registers all-terrains vehicles ("ATV"), with the exception of snowmobiles and motorcycles that are not used on public streets (Veh. & Traf. 2102).

If the decedent owned a motor vehicle and you cannot find the original certificate of title, you can apply to the local Department of Motor Vehicles for a duplicate title. The title will be issued in the name of the decedent. To get the duplicate title, you will need to complete form MV-902. You can get that form from your local the Department of Motor Vehicles or you can down-load it from their Web site.

 NYS DEPARTMENT OF MOTOR VEHICLES
http://www.nydmv.state.ny.us

Once you receive a copy of the title, it will indicate whether monies are owned on the motor vehicle. If so, the name and address of the lienholder will be listed on the title certificate. You will need to contact the lienholder and get a copy of the contract that is the basis of the loan, and the current loan balance.

THE LEASED CAR
You may find that the car is leased and not owned by the decedent. If so, contact the lessor and get a copy of the lease agreement. Check to see whether the decedent had life insurance as part of the agreement. If he did, then the lease may now be paid in full and the beneficiary of the car should be able to use the car for the remainder of the leasing period, or take title to the car, whichever option is available under the lease agreement. The Personal Representative (or the beneficiary) can send the death certificate to the leasing company with a copy of the contract and a letter requesting that the transfer be made.

If the lease is not paid in full upon the decedent's death, arrangements need to be made to satisfy the terms of the agreement. See Chapter 6 for information about transferring a leased car.

LOCATE TITLE TO MOBILE HOME

In New York, mobile homes are titled and registered in the same manner as any other motor vehicle. See the previous page if you cannot locate the certificate of title to the mobile home. If the decedent owned a parcel of land and his mobile home was permanently attached to that land, see Chapter 6 for information about transferring the land and the mobile home to the proper beneficiary.

If the decedent owned a mobile home that is kept in a leased space, you need to locate the lease to the mobile home lot. If you cannot locate the lease, contact the landlord for a copy, and proceed in the same manner as for a residential lease (see Page 68).

LOCATE TITLE TO WATERCRAFT

Title to a boat is proof of ownership of the boat. The Department of Motor Vehicles is in charge of the registration of boats that are operated on public waterways within the state. They also issue title certificates for boats at least 14' long, that are registered in New York and whose model year is 1987 or newer. If you cannot locate the title certificate to the watercraft, contact your local Department of Motor Vehicles to obtain a duplicate certificate of title.

LOCATE TITLE TO AIRCRAFT

If the decedent owned an aircraft, then you should find a certificate of title to the aircraft. The Civil Aviation Registry of the Federal Aviation Administration ("FAA") contains all of the ownership and security documents that have been filed with the FAA. If you cannot locate title to the aircraft you can contact the Civil Aviation Registry. They do not perform title searches, however they can give you a list of title search companies. If you wish to perform the title search yourself you can call the Aircraft Registration Branch at (405) 954-3116 for more information or you can visit the FAA Web site.

 THE FEDERAL AVIATION ADMINISTRATION
http://www2.faa.gov

New York State does not have any registration requirement for aircraft or pilots.

 **LAWYER**

DECEDENT'S ONGOING BUSINESS

If the decedent was the sole owner of a business, or if he owned a partnership interest in a business, the Personal Representative needs to contact the company accountant to obtain the company's business records. If there is a company attorney, he may be able to assist in obtaining the records. If you are a beneficiary of the Estate, consider consulting with your own attorney to determine what rights and responsibilities you may have in the business.

THE DECEDENT'S RESIDENTIAL LEASE

If the decedent was renting his residence, he may have a written lease agreement. It is important to locate the lease because the decedent's Estate may be responsible to make payments under the lease. If you cannot locate the lease, ask the landlord for a copy. If he reports that there was no written lease, verify that the decedent was renting on a month to month basis, and then work out a mutually agreeable time in which to vacate the premises.

If a written lease is in effect, determine the end of the lease period, and whether there was a security deposit. Ask whether the landlord will agree to cancel the lease. If not, he has the right to make a claim on the decedent's Estate for monies owed. If no one starts a Probate proceeding, after three months from the date of death, the landlord can sue the surviving spouse for monies owed by the decedent under the lease agreement. If there is no surviving spouse, the landlord can sue the children of the descendant, and if none, then anyone who is entitled to inherit the decedent's property (Real Property 711 (2)).

It is prudent to have an attorney review the lease to determine what rights and responsibilities remain in the event the landlord reports that he intends to take action to collect the balance of monies due under the lease.

COLLECT DEEDS

Collect deeds to all of the property owned by the decedent. In addition to the deed, look for other documents associated with the property, such as a mortgage. You may come across a Title Insurance policy. The new owner might be able to turn in that policy and receive a discount toward the purchase of a new title insurance, so it is important to keep the policy together with the deed.

Instead of a title insurance policy you may find an *Abstract of Title*. An Abstract of Title is a summary of the documents or facts appearing on the public record which affect title to the property. The Abstract will need to be updated once the property is transferred. We will discuss the transfer of property in Chapter 6.

Many people keep deeds in a safe deposit box. If you cannot find the deed in the decedent's home, then you need to determine whether he had a safe deposit box and if so, you need to examine the contents of the box. See the end of this chapter for information about how to access the decedent's safe deposit box.

If you know that the decedent owned real property (lot, residential property, condominium) but you cannot find the deed, contact the County Clerk in the recording department in the county where the property is located. In New York City, the Register is in charge of keeping land records. You will need to identify the parcel of land by giving the legal description of the land or its parcel identification number. You can find this information on the last tax bill sent to the decedent. If you cannot find the last tax bill, call the County Assessor's office and they will give you the information.

You can access New York City deed records on-line:
    http://a836-acris.myc.gov/scripts/docsearch.dll/index

| Special Situation | LOCATING THE OUT OF STATE DEED |

You need to locate the deed and any related document (Abstract of Title, title insurance policy, recorded condominium approval, etc.) to out of state property owned by the decedent.

THE LOST OUT OF STATE DEED

If you know the decedent owned out of state real property, but cannot find the deed, you can use the same procedure just described, namely, you can check with the recording department in the county where the property is located. In some states, the Clerk of the Circuit Court is in charge of the recording department. In other states it may be the County Recorder or Registrar of Deeds. The Clerk in the recording department should be able to give you a copy of the last recorded deed.

Many states index the property by the name of the current owner of the property, so if you know the county where the property is located, you should be able to find the deed by giving the decedent's name to the Clerk.

If you do not know the county in which the property is located, you will need to wait for the next tax bill. In many states the tax bill contains its legal description, or tax identification number.

COLLECT TAX RECORDS

The decedent's final state and federal income tax returns need to be filed so you should locate all of his tax records for the past three years. If you cannot locate his prior tax records, check his personal telephone book and/or his personal bank register to see if he employed someone to prepare his taxes. If you can locate his tax preparer, then he should have a copy of those records.

If you are unable to locate the decedent's federal tax returns, they can be obtained from the IRS. The IRS will send copies of the decedent's tax filings to anyone who has a *fiduciary relationship* with the decedent. The IRS considers the following people to be a fiduciary:
- ➤ the person appointed as the Personal Representative of the decedent's Estate
- ➤ the Successor Trustee of the decedent's Trust
- ➤ if the person died intestate (without a Will), whoever is legally entitled to possession of the decedent's property (See Chapter 5 for an explanation of the Rules Governing Intestate Succession).

The fiduciary can receive copies of the decedent's tax filings by notifying IRS that he/she is acting in a fiduciary capacity, and then requesting the copies.

To notify the IRS of the fiduciary capacity file Form 56: NOTICE CONCERNING FIDUCIARY RELATIONSHIP

Your accountant can file these forms for you or you can obtain the forms from the IRS by calling (800) 829-3676 or you can download them from the FORMS section of the IRS Web site.

 INTERNAL REVENUE SERVICE
http://www.irs.gov

LOCATE STATE INCOME TAX RETURN

If you cannot locate the decedent's state income tax return you can get copies from the New York State Income Tax department by calling (800) 225-5829 or you can write to:

New York State Income Tax
Centralized Photocopy Unit
W.A. Harriman Campus, Bldg.8
Albany, NY 12227

As with the IRS, the state will require some proof of a fiduciary relationship from the person making the request. They will also request the decedent's social security number and the last address that he used to file his return.

You can obtain information about New York State Taxes from the New York State Income Tax Web Site. The web site contains tax forms that you can download.

 NEW YORK STATE INCOME TAX
http://www.tax.state.ny.us/

LOCATE OUT OF STATE ACCOUNTS

If the decedent had out of state bank or brokerage accounts, then you might be able to locate them if they mail out monthly or quarterly statements. Not all financial institutions do so, but all institutions are required to send out an IRS tax form 1099 each year giving the amount of interest earned on that account. Once the forms come in, you will learn the location of all of the decedent's active accounts.

If the decedent was forgetful, he may have money in a lost bank account or abandoned safe deposit box. Property that is unclaimed is turned over to the New York State Comptroller after a period of time as set by New York law. The time period depends on the item:

⧗　1 year for unclaimed wages (Aband. Prop. 1308)

⧗　2 years after service is discontinued
for an unclaimed utility deposit (Aband. Prop. 400)

⧗　3 years after monies are payable under a life
insurance policy (Aband. Prop. 700)

⧗　5 years for the last transaction on a bank account
(Aband. Prop. 300)

⧗　15 years from the date of issue of a travelers check
or a money order (Aband. Prop. 1309).

The Comptroller will try to locate the owner of the property. If a tangible item (such as jewelry) remains unclaimed, he will convert it to cash by holding a public auction. If the owner (or his heirs) later claims the item, they will receive the proceeds of the sale (Aband. Prop. 1403). To determine whether the decedent is the owner of unclaimed property call (518) 270-2200 (in state (800) 221-9311). You can also get information from Comptroller's Web site.

 OFFICE OF THE STATE COMPTROLLER
http://www.osc.state.ny.us

CLAIMS FOR DECEDENT VICTIMS OF HOLOCAUST
The New York State Banking Department has a special Claims Processing Office for Holocaust survivors or their heirs. The office processes claims for Swiss bank accounts that were dormant since the end of World War II. If the decedent was a victim of the Holocaust, you can get information about money that may be due to the decedent's Estate by calling (800) 695-3318.

CLAIMS IN OTHER STATES

Each state has an agency or department that is responsible for handling lost, abandoned or unclaimed property located within that state. If the decedent had residences in other states, call the UNCLAIMED PROPERTY department of the state Comptroller or Treasurer to see if the decedent has unclaimed property in that state. EAGLE PUBLISHING COMPANY OF BOCA lists telephone numbers for the unclaimed property division for each state at the Public Information section of their Web site.

http://www.eaglepublishing.com

CLAIMS FOR INCOME TAX REFUNDS

The IRS reports that each year some 2 million taxpayers fail to claim some 3 billion dollars in refunds. Some employees had taxes withheld from their wages but had too little income to file a tax return and may not be aware that the taxes they paid are refundable. Other employees may not have had any tax withheld, but they might be eligible for the refundable Earned Income Tax Credit. The IRS gives taxpayers five years to claim these funds. You can determine whether they are holding a check for the decedent by calling the IRS at (800) 829-1040. You can get more information about unclaimed tax refunds by visiting the IRS Web site. http://www.irs.gov/

UNCLAIMED STATE TAX REFUNDS

The New York Department of Taxation and Finance also reports that thousands of tax refunds are returned to them each year by the U.S. Postal Service marked "undeliverable." You can call them at (800) 443-3200 to determine whether there is an unclaimed check for the decedent; or you can search their Web site.

 NY DEPARTMENT OF TAXATION AND FINANCE
http://www.tax.state.ny.us

THE LOST PENSION

The decedent may be entitled to benefits under a pension plan of a prior employer. If the decedent worked for an employer for any significant period of time, say 5 years or more, then you need to check with the company benefit representative to determine whether any pension funds are payable. If you are unable to locate the former employer, then it could be that the company moved or merged with another company. There are several ways to track down the company, starting with the Secretary of State to learn of the company's current status (see page 48).

CONTACT THE UNION If company workers belonged to a union, you can contact the union and they may be able to help you locate the company; or tell you what happened to the pension funds.

CONTACT SOCIAL SECURITY The Social Security Administration has the decedent's work record and the employer identification number for each of his employers. The Personal Representative should be able to get that information by calling the Social Security Administration at (800) 772-1213. Using the employer identification number you might be able to determine whether the pension fund was taken over by another company.

RESEARCH THE INTERNET Pension Benefit Guaranty Corporation insures private sector pensions. They operate an on-line search tool for those employees whose pension plans were closed because of bankruptcy, or because the company dissolved the plan, or because the company could not locate the employee. You can search their Web site by employee name or by the company name.

PENSION BENEFIT GUARANTY CORPORATION
http://www.pbgc.gov/search

LOCATE CONTRACTS

If the decedent belonged to a health club or gym, he may have prepaid for the year. Look for the club contract. It will give the terms of the agreement. If you cannot locate the contract, contact the company for a copy of the agreement. If the contract was prepaid, determine whether the agreement provides for a refund for the unused portion.

Even if the contract does not provide for a refund, you may be able to get the owner of the gym to agree to assigning the remaining membership to an heir of the decedent's Estate. Such an assignment is good public relations as well as a means of generating new business should the heir decide to purchase his own membership.

SERVICE CONTRACT

Many people purchase appliance service contracts to have their appliances serviced in the event that an appliance should need repair. If the decedent had a security system then he may have had a service contract with a company to monitor the system and contact the police in the event of a break-in.

If the decedent had a service contract, you need to locate it and determine whether it can be assigned to the new owner of the property. If the contract is assignable, the new owner can reimburse the decedent's Estate for the unused portion. If the contract cannot be assigned, then once the property is transferred, try to obtain a refund for the unused portion of the contract.

FILING THE WILL

Anyone who has possession of the decedent's original Will should deposit it with the Clerk of the Surrogate's Court in the county of the decedent's residence. If the decedent owned property in New York, but did not live here, the Will can be deposited with the Clerk in the county where the decedent's property is located.

There is only one original Will, so it is important to hand carry the original document to Court. If you have the Will but are unable to make the delivery in person, you can mail it to the Court, but send it by certified mail so that you will have proof of delivery. Make a copy of the Will for your own records before delivering or mailing it to the Court.

If you are the Personal Representative of the Will, you can give it to your attorney to file with the Court as part of the Probate proceeding. If you do not have the Will but believe someone has it in their possession, or perhaps may have even destroyed the Will, you have the right to ask the Surrogate's Court to require that person to come before the Court and be questioned about the matter. You will need to employ an attorney who is experienced in Probate matters to file the petition asking the Court to compel that person to either produce the Will or give testimony about the location of the Will. If the Court finds the person did not have good reason to withhold the Will, he can require that person to pay your attorney fees (Surr. Ct. Proc. Act 1401).

 **LAWYER**

PROBATING
OUT OF STATE PROPERTY

If the decedent had his residence in New York and owned property in another state, you may need to conduct the initial Probate in New York and an *ancillary* (secondary) Probate in the other state. If the decedent had his residence in another state and owned property in New York, it may need to be the other way around; namely, you may need to conduct the initial Probate in the other state (Surr. Ct. Proc. Act 1602).

If you are going to be Personal Representative, and the decedent owned property in another state or was a resident of another state, before depositing the Will with the Court consult with an experienced Probate attorney <u>in each state</u> to determine where the initial Probate should be conducted. Convenience is important, but there are other things you need to consider:

COST OF PROBATE
Ask each attorney whether the location of the initial Probate procedure will have an effect on the total cost of Probate.

WHO INHERITS THE INTESTATE ESTATE
Intestate laws vary significantly state to state. If the decedent died without a Will, it is important to determine whether the location of the initial Probate procedure will change the amount each heir will inherit.

ESTATE/INHERITANCE TAXES
Determine whether the location of the initial procedure will have an impact on the amount of taxes that need to be paid.

> **Special Situation** WILL DRAFTED IN ANOTHER STATE OR COUNTRY
>
> A Will that was drafted in another state or country can be accepted into Probate in New York, provided:
>
> ☑ the Will was prepared and signed in accordance with New York law - or -
>
> ☑ the Will was prepared and signed according to the laws of the state where it was drafted - or -
>
> ☑ the Will was prepared and signed according to the laws of the state of the decedent's residence (Est. Powers & Trusts 3-5.1).
>
> See Chapter 5 for a discussion of what constitutes a valid Will in the state of New York.

THE MISSING WILL

People tend to put off making a Will until they think they need to. For many, that need arises when they are elderly and/or seriously ill and have property that they want to leave to someone. It is uncommon for a young person to have a Will; but those who are aged, and with significant assets, usually have one. A survey conducted for the American Association of Retired Persons ("AARP") found that the probability of having a Will increases with age. Forty-four percent of those surveyed who were between the ages of 50 to 54 had a Will. This increased to 85% for those 80 and older. You can find details of the survey at the AARP Web site.

 AMERICAN ASSOCIATION OF RETIRED PERSONS
http://research.aarp.org

LOCATING THE WILL

Those who make a Will usually tell the person they appoint as Executor of the existence of the Will. Chances are that someone in the decedent's circle of family and friends knows whether there is a Will. If you believe that the decedent had a Will, but you cannot find it, then there are at least three places to check out:

⇨ **THE DECEDENT'S ATTORNEY**

Look at the decedent's checkbook for the past few years and see whether he paid any attorney fees. If you are able to locate the decedent's attorney, call and inquire whether the attorney ever drafted a Will for the decedent, and if so, whether the attorney has the original Will in his possession. If he has the Will, then ask him to forward it to the Surrogate's Court in the county of the decedent's residence. Asking the attorney to forward the Will to the Court does not obligate you to employ the attorney should you later find that you need the assistance of an attorney for the Probate administration.

⇨ **THE CLERK OF THE PROBATE COURT**

As explained, New York law requires that whoever has the original Will deposit it with the Probate Court as soon as that person learns of the death (Surr. Ct. Proc. Act 1401). It is a good idea to check with the Clerk in the county where the decedent lived in the chance that someone found the Will and filed it with the Court.

⇨ **THE SAFE DEPOSIT BOX**

Most people keep their original Will in a safe deposit box. If you believe that the decedent had a Will but you cannot find it, check to see if the decedent had a safe deposit box. If he did, you will need to gain entry to that box to see whether the Will is in the box. See Page 82 for an explanation of how to gain entry to the safe deposit box.

 **LAWYER** | A COPY OF THE WILL AND NO ORIGINAL

A person can revoke his Will simply by destroying it i.e., by ripping it up, or by writing over it in such a manner as to indicate that the Will is cancelled or revoked (Est. Powers & Trusts 3-4.1). If you have a copy of the Will and cannot find the original, the Probate Judge will presume that the decedent revoked his Will by destroying it. If you believe the original was not revoked but is lost, you can ask the Probate Court to admit a copy of the Will to Probate.

New York courts have allowed a lost Will to be probated provided it can be proven that

☑ the Will was not revoked, AND

☑ the Will was signed according to New York law, namely that the Will maker signed his name at the end of the Will in the presence of at least two witness who can testify that they saw the Will maker sign the Will and that he was competent to make a Will (Est. Powers & Trusts 3-2.1), AND

☑ all of the provisions of the Will are clearly proved by the witnesses, or by a true copy of the Will (Surr. Ct. Proc. Act 1407).

These are not easy things to prove. If you wish to have a lost Will admitted to Probate, you will need to employ an attorney experienced in Probate matters to present your case to the Court.

ACCESSING THE SAFE DEPOSIT BOX

Once you notify a bank in New York that the lessee of a safe deposit box is dead, they will seal the box and not allow anyone to access the box until they receive a Court order authorizing someone to examine the contents of the box. If the decedent rented a safe deposit box jointly with another person, or if he gave someone authority to access the safe deposit box, the bank will allow that person to examine the contents of the box in the presence of an officer of the bank. The bank will allow the joint tenant or the decedent's agent to make a copy of any burial instruction or deed to a cemetery plot; however they will not allow the original document to be removed without a Court order (Surr. Ct. Proc. Act 2003).

If a Probate proceeding is necessary, the person appointed as Personal Representative will have authority to take possession of the contents of the safe deposit box. If you do not think that Probate will be necessary, you can go to the Surrogate's Court in the county of the decedent's residence and ask the Clerk to assist you in asking the judge to issue an order allowing you to do the following:

⇨ examine the contents of the safe deposit box in the presence of an officer of the bank

⇨ take an inventory of the contents of the box

⇨ take possession of the deed to the decedent's burial plot

⇨ have the officer deliver the decedent's Will to the Clerk of the Surrogate's Court, either in person or by certified mail

⇨ have the officer deliver the decedent's life insurance policy to the named beneficiary.

If you find other valuables in the box that need to be removed from the box, you will need to go through some kind of Probate procedure to get possession of those items. See Chapter 6 for an explanation of what type of Probate procedure may be necessary in order to get possession of the contents of the decedent's safe deposit box.

Once you have located the decedent's property you may think the next step is to determine who gets to inherit that property. But some of that property may be needed to pay monies owed by the decedent; so the next step is to determine what, if any, bills need to be paid.

And that is the topic of the next chapter.

What Bills Need To Be Paid? 4

The Personal Representative has the duty to be sure that all valid claims against the Estate (demands for payment) are paid. If the decedent had debts, but no money or property, then of course, there is no way to pay the claim. The only remaining question is whether anyone else is responsible to pay for the monies owed. If the decedent was married, the first person the creditor will look to is the decedent's spouse. To understand the basis of this expectation, you need to know a bit of the history of our legal system.

Our laws are derived from the English Common Law. Under early English Common Law, a single woman had the right to own property in her own name and also the right to contract to buy or sell property; but when she married, her legal identity merged with her spouse. She could not hold property free from her husband's claim or control. She could no longer enter into a contract without her husband's permission.

Once married, a woman became financially dependent on her husband. He, in turn, became legally responsible to provide his wife with basic necessities — food, clothing, shelter and medical services. If anyone provided basic necessities to his wife, then regardless of whether the husband agreed to be responsible for the debt, he became obliged to pay for them. This law was called the DOCTRINE OF NECESSARIES.

States in America departed from English Common Law by enacting a series of Married Women's Rights Acts. The New York legislature passed a Married Woman Rights law giving a married woman the right to own property, to make contracts and run a business in the same manner as any single woman (Gen. Oblig. Law 3-301).

Court cases followed that tested whether the Doctrine of Necessaries still applied. Judges had to decide:

If a wife can own property and contract to pay for her own necessities, should her husband be responsible for such debts in the event she does not have enough money to pay for them?

And if it is determined that the husband is responsible for his wife's necessities, should she be responsible for his?

Some states decided to make the Doctrine of Necessaries part of their state law. Other states, such as New Jersey, decided to apply the Doctrine equally to both sexes, making the husband responsible to pay for his wife's necessities and the wife responsible to pay for her husband's necessities. Other states abolished the law altogether. For example, in Florida, courts have ruled that a creditor cannot collect from the spouse unless the spouse agreed to pay the debt.

In New York, the Doctrine was not made part of the state law, however New York courts have ruled that if a creditor cannot collect payment for necessities from the debtor, the creditor can require payment from his or her spouse (*Our Lady of Lourdes Memorial Hospital, Inc. v. Frey.*, 152 A.D.2d 73, 548 N.Y.S.2d 109 (1989)). Which leads to the next question. Is anyone other than your spouse responsible to pay monies you owe? For joint debts, the answer is "yes."

JOINT DEBTS

A *joint debt* is a debt that two or more people are responsible to pay. Usually the contract or promissory note states that the parties agree to *joint and several liability*, meaning they all agree to pay the debt and each of them promises to be personally responsible to pay the debt. A joint debt can also be in the form of monies owed by one person with payment guaranteed by another person. If the person who owes the money does not pay, the *guarantor* (the person who guaranteed payment) is responsible to make payment. Funeral expenses, legal fees to Probate the decedent's Estate are all debts of his Estate. They are not joint debts unless someone guaranteed payment for monies owed.

PAYING FOR THE JOINT DEBT

If another person is jointly responsible for monies owed by the decedent, then that bill should be paid from any joint account held with the decedent. If the joint debtor did not have a joint account with the decedent, then the joint debtor must pay the bill from his/her own funds.

SPOUSE JOINT SPOUSAL DEBTS

Loans signed by the decedent and his spouse are joint debts, as are charges on credit cards that both were authorized to use. Property taxes are a joint debt if the decedent and the spouse both owned the property. Also, if the decedent received Medicaid for his health care needs when he was 55 or older, the surviving spouse can be held liable to reimburse the state for monies spent on his behalf (Social Services Law 366).

Suppose all of the decedent's funds are held jointly with a family member and the joint owner of the bank account did not agree to pay those debts? Can the creditor require that half of the joint funds be set aside to pay the debt? The answer depends on how the account was set up. If the account was set up with *rights of survivorship*, the surviving owner owns all of the money in the account as of the date of death. If it was set up as a *Tenancy In Common*, with no right of survivorship, the creditor can demand payment from the decedent's share of the account.

Under New York law, unless the bank account states otherwise, it is presumed that a deposit account (including CD's) in two or more names, is Tenancy In Common (Est. Powers & Trusts 6-2.2(a)). As soon as the bank is notified of the death, they will freeze an account held as a Tenancy In Common until a Personal Representative is appointed and takes possession of the decedent's share of the account.

If the account is held jointly with rights of survivorship, as of the date of death, the survivor owns everything in the account. Still, he may be required to contribute account funds for taxes or to settle the decedent's Estate. Specifically, the decedent's share of a joint account is included as part of his *Taxable Estate*. The surviving owner may be required to pay whatever taxes are due on the share of the account that he inherited. In addition, the Personal Representative has the right to ask for as much of the decedent's share of the account as is necessary to settle his Estate (Est. Powers & Trusts 2-1.8, 12-1.2).

If the decedent owed money then the debt needs to be paid from assets owned by the decedent — which leads to the next question "Did the decedent have any money in his own name when he died?"

If the decedent died without any money or property in his name, then there is no money to pay any creditor. The only question that remains is whether anyone else is liable to pay those bills. The issue of payment most often arises in relation to services provided by nursing homes. When a person enters a nursing home, he is usually too ill to speak for himself or even sign his name. In such cases, the nursing home administrator will ask the spouse or a family member to sign a battery of papers on behalf of the patient before allowing the patient to enter the facility. Buried in that battery of papers may be a statement that the family member agrees to be responsible for payment to the nursing home. If the family member refuses to guarantee payment and the patient's finances are limited, then the facility may refuse to admit the patient.

Under the Federal Nursing Home Reform Law, a nursing home that accepts Medicare or Medicaid payments is prohibited from requiring a family member to guarantee payment as a condition of allowing the patient to enter that facility (USC Title 42 §1395i-3(c)(5)(A)(ii)). Nonetheless, it is common practice for a nursing home, in effect, to say "Either someone agrees to pay for the patient's bill or you need to find a different facility."

Their position is understandable, in light of the fact that even if the patient is married, the nursing home cannot require payment from the spouse unless the spouse agrees to be responsible for monies owed. Most nursing homes are business establishments and not charitable organizations. Even not-for-profit organizations must cover their costs. The nursing home must be paid for the services they provide or they soon will be out of business. For an insolvent patient, the solution is to have the patient admitted to the facility as a Medicaid patient.

But suppose the decedent had some money when he entered the nursing home and you agreed to guarantee payment to the nursing home. What if you feel that you were coerced into signing as a guarantor?

Are you now liable to pay the decedent's final nursing home bill if your family member died without funds?

An experienced Elder Law attorney will be able to answer these questions after examining the documents that you signed and the conditions under which the patient entered the nursing home.

PAYING THE DECEDENT'S BILLS

If the decedent was married and no Probate procedure is necessary, then the surviving spouse needs to make provision for paying bills they were both responsible to pay. If the decedent was not married and he owned property belonging to him alone, such as a bank account, securities or real property, then paying monies owed by the decedent falls to the Personal Representative.

Just as soon as he is appointed, the Personal Representative is required to make a diligent effort to locate all of the decedent's creditors and notify them that they have the right to file a claim against the decedent's Estate. Any creditor who is not given notice has seven months from the day the Personal Representative was appointed to come forward and present his claim (Surr. Ct. Proc. Act 1802).

The Personal Representative needs to look over each claim and decide whether that claim is valid. The problem with making that decision is that the decedent is not here to say whether he actually received the goods and services that are now being billed to his Estate.

That is especially the case for medical or nursing care bills. An example of improper billing brought to the attention of this author was that of a bill submitted for a physical examination of the decedent. The bill listed the date of the examination as July 10th, but the decedent died on July 9th. Other incorrect billings may not be as obvious, so each invoice needs to be carefully examined.

If the Personal Representative decides to challenge a bill, and is unable to settle the matter with the creditor, then the Probate Court will decide whether the debt is valid and should be paid.

MEDICAL BILLS COVERED BY INSURANCE

If the decedent had health insurance you may receive an invoice stamped "THIS IS NOT A BILL." This means the health care provider has submitted the bill to the decedent's health insurance company and expects to be paid by them. If the decedent was receiving Medicare, you will receive a **Medicare Summary Notice** listing all of the services or supplies that were billed to Medicare for the prior 30 days. In some areas of the country, you can get a copy of the decedent's Medicare Summary Notice from the Internet. To see if it is available in your area, look up e-MSN in the "Frequently Asked Questions" section of the Medicare Web site http://www.medicare.gov.

Even though payment is not requested, it is important to verify that the bill is valid for two reasons:

➢   **LATER LIABILITY**

If the insurer refuses to pay the claim, the facility will seek payment from whoever is in possession of the decedent's property, and that may reduce the amount inherited by the beneficiaries.

➢   **INCREASED HEALTH CARE COSTS**

Regardless of whether the decedent was covered by a private health care insurer or Medicare, improper billing increases the cost of health insurance to all of us. Consumers pay high premiums for health coverage. We, as taxpayers, all share the cost of Medicare. If unnecessary or fraudulent billing is not checked, then ultimately, we all pay.

If you believe that you have come across a case of Medicare fraud, you can call the ANTI-FRAUD HOTLINE (800) 447-8477 and report the incident to the Office of the Inspector General of the United States Department of Health and Human Services.

HOW TO CHECK MEDICARE BILLING

The structure of Medicare has changed giving people in some parts of the country the option of staying with the *Original Medicare Plan* or choosing one of the *Medicare Advantage Plans*. Health care coverage depends on which plan is chosen. If the decedent was covered by Medicare, you need to determine whether he was covered under the Original Medicare Plan, or whether he chose a Medicare Advantage Plan. The publication *Medicare and You* explains coverage under the different options. See page 51 to obtain a copy of the booklet.

Coverage under a Medicare Advantage Plan is explained in the membership materials given to the decedent at the time he signed up for the plan.

BILLING UNDER THE ORIGINAL MEDICARE PLAN

ASSIGNMENT

An important billing question for those under the Original Medicare Plan is whether the health care provider agreed to accept Medicare *assignment*, meaning that they agreed to accept the Medicare-approved amount. If so, the patient is responsible for the coinsurance rate (usually 20% of the approved amount) and any deductible amount. Doctors and health care providers who do not accept assignment, are limited in the amount they can charge for a Medicare covered service. The highest they can charge is **15%** over the Medicare-approved amount. This *Limiting Charge* applies only to certain services and does not apply to supplies and equipment. For more information about assignment you can call (800) 633-4227 for your free copy of *Does your doctor or supplier accept "assignment?"* or you can down-load the publication from the Medicare Web site:
http://www.medicare.gov

ADVANCE BENEFICIARY NOTICE

For those who are in the Original Medicare Plan, a doctor or a supplier may give notice saying that Medicare probably will not pay for the service that is about to be provided. This is called an *Advance Beneficiary Notice*. If the patient still wants the service after receiving such Notice, he will be asked to sign an agreement stating that he will pay for the service, in the event that Medicare does not pay.

If all of this appears confusing, it is.

To check the decedent's Medicare billing, you need the answers to the following questions:

What is the plan?

Determine whether the decedent was in the Original Medicare Plan or in one of the Medicare Advantage Plans.

What is covered under the plan?

The *Medicare and You* booklet explains what is covered under the Original Medicare Plan. You will need a copy of the membership materials for the Medicare Advantage Plans to determine what is covered under that plan.

Does the Provider accept Assignment?

If the decedent was in the Original Medicare Plan, you need to determine whether the health care provider accepted assignment; and if not whether the Limiting Charge applies to the services provided. If assignment is accepted or the Limiting Charge applies, you need to determine the Medicare-approved amount.

Did the decedent agree to pay?

If the decedent was in the Original Medicare Plan, check to see whether the decedent was given an Advance Beneficiary Notice; and if so, whether he signed a contract agreeing to pay in the event that Medicare refuses to pay.

If the health care provider reports to you that a service provided to the decedent is not covered by Medicare, or if the facility submits the bill and Medicare refuses to pay, check to see if you agree with that ruling by finding answers to the questions on the prior page. You can appeal that decision if you believe that the decedent was wrongly denied coverage.

If the decedent was in the Original Medicare Plan, you will find information about how to file an appeal on the Medicare Summary Notice. If he was part of the Medicare Advantage, you will find that information in his health care plan materials. The book *Your Medicare Rights and Protections* (CMS Pub. No. 10112) contains information about appeals. You can get a free copy by calling (800) 633-4227 or by down-loading it from the Medicare Web site.   **www.medicare.gov.**

As of July, 2005, the U.S. Department of Health and Human Services will be in charge of Medicare Appeals. They will hold hearings with video conference equipment or by telephone. They will allow the beneficiary to appeal in person before a judge only if "special or extraordinary circumstances exist." Even if an in-person hearing is allowed, judges will be available in only four locations Miami, Florida, Cleveland, Ohio, Irvine, California and Arlington, Virginia. Beneficiaries who insist on a face-to-face hearing will lose their right to receive a decision within 90 days, so it may take considerable time before the matter is settled.

GETTING HELP WITH THE APPEAL

You can appeal the decision yourself, but it is best to first call **THE MEDICARE RIGHTS CENTER** at (800) 333-4114 to learn of your rights. This agency is a private, nonprofit, organization partially funded by the **NEW YORK STATE OFFICE OF THE AGING**. They offer Medicare counseling without charge.

If you want an attorney to assist with your appeal, call your local Bar Association for a referral to an attorney experienced in Medicare appeals (see Page xiii) . Some attorneys work *pro bono* (literally for the public good; i.e. without charge) but most charge to assist in an appeal. Federal statute 42 U.S.C. 406(a)(2)(A) limits the amount an attorney may charge for a successful Medicare appeal to 25% of the amount recovered or $4,000, whichever is the smaller amount.

Medicaid is a program that provides medical and long term nursing care for people with low income and limited resources. The program is funded jointly by the federal and state government. Federal law requires the state to recover monies spent from the Estate of a Medicaid recipient who was 55 or older when the decedent received Medicaid assistance. The state will seek reimbursement for the cost of nursing home care or for home based care or for other community based services (42 U.S.C. 1396(p)).

There usually is no money to recover because to qualify for Medicaid in New York, a person may not have more than $4,000 (as of the year 2005) in assets. But sometimes it happens that the person on Medicaid dies and his Estate later receives money perhaps as part of the settlement of a lawsuit — or he may have owned a home in his name only. Owning a home does not disqualify a person from receiving Medicaid, however if he received Medicaid benefits after age 55, the state has the right to place a lien on that home and seek recovery from the proceeds of the sale of the house once he dies. Federal law prohibits any recovery of monies, until the surviving spouse, and/or disabled child, of the decedent are deceased.

The Personal Representative will need to notify the state that they have a right to file a claim against the Estate to recover monies spent for the benefit of the decedent. The decedent's caseworker can give him information about who to notify that there is a Probate proceeding being conducted to distribute the decedent's assets.

SOME THINGS ARE CREDITOR PROOF

Sometimes it happens that the decedent had money or property titled in his name only, but he also had a significant amount of debt. In such cases the beneficiaries may wonder whether they should go through a Probate procedure if there will be little, if anything, left after the creditors are paid. Before making the decision consider that some assets are protected under New York law:

✧ PENSION PLANS ✧

Annuities, pensions, profit sharing or other retirement plans regulated by the federal Employee Retirement Income Security Act of 1974 ("ERISA"), including plans identified by the Internal Revenue Code as 401, 402(a)5, 403(a)(4), 408 A or 408 (d)(3) (IRA and Keogh accounts) are creditor proof (C.P.L.R. 5205(c)(2)). Monies received by a beneficiary of such plans are protected from the decedent's creditors with the following exceptions:

NO EXEMPTION FOR TAXES

In general, income taxes are not paid when money is placed in a retirement plan. Taxes are paid when the monies are withdrawn from the account regardless of whether the monies are withdrawn by the retiree or the person he named as beneficiary of the retirement plan. If you are inheriting money from the decedent's pension, retirement allowance, or annuity, you may need to pay taxes on those monies. You should consult with an accountant or an attorney to determine how much money needs to be set aside to pay for federal and state income taxes.

✧ EXEMPTIONS FOR SURVIVING SPOUSE ✧

The decedent's surviving spouse and/or minor children are entitled to take certain items of the decedent's Estate free from the claims of any of his creditors.

THE HOMESTEAD EXEMPTION

New York property owned and occupied by a person as his main residence is called **homestead** property. The **equity** in the homestead is the current value of the property less monies owed on the property. If there is less than $10,000 equity in the property, no creditor can force the sale of the property (C.P.L.R. 5206). There are exceptions to this rule. Creditor protection does not extend to delinquent taxes or mortgages.

If there is more than $10,000 worth of equity in the homestead, the creditor can force the sale of the property to pay for monies owed. If the property is sold, the first $10,000 of the proceeds of the sale goes to the owner as his Homestead Exemption.

If the decedent owned his home in his name only, his Homestead Exemption continues for the surviving spouse and minor child — but only until the spouse dies and the homeowner's children have all reached the age of 18. This means that if the home equity is less than $10,000, should the owner of the property die, his creditors cannot force the sale of the homestead while it is occupied by the homeowner's surviving spouse or minor child.

Of course, if the deceased homeowner was single, and without minor children, the Homestead Exemption is lost. The creditor can ask the Probate Court to have the homestead sold in order to pay the decedent's debts .

✦ EXEMPT PERSONAL PROPERTY ✦

If a person has his principal residence in New York, upon his death the following items become the property of his surviving spouse, free from the claims of his creditors:

(1) all household furniture, appliances, computers, musical instruments and furnishings used in and about the house, up to $10,000 in value

(2) the family bible, family pictures, video tapes, computer discs, software and books, not exceeding $1,000 in value

(3) domestic animals and necessary food for 60 days, farm machinery, one tractor and one lawn tractor, not exceeding $15,000 in value

(4) one motor vehicle not exceeding $15,000 in value. The spouse can elect to take cash instead of the decedent's motor vehicle (up to $15,000). If the decedent owned more than one vehicle, then the spouse has his/her choice of motor vehicle. If the vehicle chosen is worth more than $15,000 the spouse must pay the difference to the Estate.

(5) money or other personal property not exceeding $15,000 in value, except if there is not enough money to pay for the funeral. In that case the funeral must be paid and the balance of the $15,000 goes to the surviving spouse (Est. Powers & Trusts 5-3.1).

The exempt values of any of these items do not include monies owed on them. For example if a car is worth $20,000 and there is a loan of $5,000, the car is worth $15,000 and it qualifies as an exempt item.

If the items described in (1) to (4) are not in existence, no substitutions of money or property can be made.

These five items are called EXEMPT PROPERTY because in a Probate proceeding the surviving spouse may ask the Court to exempt these items from the claims of creditors — except for monies owed on the item. For example, if money is owed on the car, the spouse needs to pay off the loan, otherwise the lender is entitled to repossess the car.

If there is no surviving spouse, but the decedent left children under the age of 21, they are entitled to share these exemptions between them.

None of these items are exempt from the claims of creditors, if the decedent was single, with no children under the age of 21 (Est. Powers & Trusts 5-3.1).

✧ LIFE INSURANCE PROCEEDS ✧

Insurance proceeds from a life insurance policy or an annuity contract are exempt from the claims of the decedent's creditors, however if the proceeds of the policy are payable to the decedent or to his Estate, those proceeds become part of his Probate Estate and are available to pay his debts (Insur. 3212).

✧ THERE IS A PRIORITY OF PAYMENT ✧

Next, consider that not all Probate debts are equal. If there are insufficient funds in the Probate Estate to pay for all claims against the decedent's Estate, then New York Statute (Surr. Ct. Proc. Act 1811) establishes an order of priority for payment:

CLASS 1: COST AND EXPENSES OF ADMINISTRATION

The cost of the Probate procedure, including filing fees, and fees charged by the Personal Representative and his attorney, must be satisfied before any other debt can be paid.

CLASS 2: REASONABLE FUNERAL EXPENSES

Second in priority are the decedent's reasonable funeral expenses. This includes the cost of the funeral, the burial lot, a suitable monument and perpetual care of the burial site.

CLASS 3: TAXES

Any debt that has preference under federal or state law. This includes Estate and income taxes and other monies owed by the decedent to the state or federal government.

CLASS 4: PROPERTY TAXES

If the decedent owned real property and taxes were assessed on that property prior to his death, then the Personal Representative must pay that tax. Whoever inherits that property must reimburse the Personal Representative unless the decedent's Will requires the taxes be paid from the Probate estate.

CLASS 5: JUDGMENTS

Judgments against the decedent are paid in chronological order, i.e., the judgment with the earliest date is the first to be paid. If any money is left, then the judgment with the next earliest date is paid, etc.

CLASS 6: ALL OTHER DEBTS

If any money is left after all the prior classes are paid, then the Personal Representative will use it to pay all of the decedent's valid debts.

Except for Class 5, there is no order of priority for any other class of debt. All the debtors in a given class have the same right to be paid. If there is not enough money to pay all of the creditors in a given class, the Personal Representative will prorate the available funds.

If the monies owed on a Class 6 debt are secured by collateral, for example a loan on a car or a mortgage on real property, then the Personal Representative can ask the Court to allow the collateral to be given to the creditor as partial or complete satisfaction of the debt.

If there is any dispute about the payment of a debt, the Probate Court will decide who is to be paid and how much they will receive.

There are federal and state laws that set time periods for pursuing a claim. Anyone who wishes to take Court action must do so within the time set by the given Statute of Limitation. For example, a law suit for the wrongful death of the decedent must be filed within two years of the death (Est. Powers & Trusts 5-4.1).

There is a Statute of Limitations for a creditor to come forward and make a claim against the decedent's Estate for monies owed. The Personal Representative must inform the decedent's creditors that the decedent died, and that a Probate proceeding is in progress. If a creditor does not file his claim within seven months from the date of the appointment of the Personal Representative, the Personal Representative is not responsible for monies he paid out in good faith before learning of the debt (Surr. Ct. Proc. Act 1802).

If the decedent owed money, and no one starts a Probate proceeding, then after 18 months, the creditor can sue in civil Court to force the beneficiary of the decedent's property to either pay the debt or sell the property and use the proceeds from the sale to satisfy that debt.

If the decedent was sued prior to his death and has a judgment that was placed against his real property, that lien continues for two years after the decedent's death, or 10 years after the filing of the judgment-roll, which ever is later (C.P.L.R. 5208). During that time, the creditor can start a civil Court action to force the beneficiary of that property to either pay the debt or sell the property and use the proceeds to pay the judgment. Bottom line, if the decedent had property in his name only, even if you do not start a Probate proceeding, a creditor can ask the Court to order that the decedent's property be sold to pay the debt.

MONIES OWED TO THE DECEDENT

Suppose you owed money to the decedent. Do you need to pay that debt now that he is dead? That depends on whether there is some written document that says the debt is forgiven once the decedent dies. For example, suppose the decedent loaned you money to buy your home. If he left a Will saying that once he dies, your debt is forgiven, you do not need to make any more payments. If you signed a promissory note and mortgage at the time you borrowed the money from the decedent, the Personal Representative should sign the original promissory note **PAID IN FULL** and return the note to you. If the mortgage was recorded, the Personal Representative needs to have a Satisfaction of Mortgage recorded in the county where the property is located. You should receive the recorded Satisfaction for your records.

If you owed the decedent money and there is no Will, or if there is a Will, and no mention of forgiving the debt, then you still owe the money. Monies borrowed from the decedent and his spouse need to be repaid to the spouse. Monies borrowed from the decedent only, become an asset to the Estate of the decedent, meaning that you owe the money to the decedent's Estate. If you are one of the beneficiaries of the Estate, you can deduct the money from your inheritance.

For example, suppose your father left $70,000 in a bank account to be divided equally between you and your brother. If you owed your father $20,000, your father's Estate is really worth $90,000 with each child entitled to $45,000. Instead of paying the $20,000, you can agree to receive $25,000 and have the $20,000 debt forgiven. Your brother will receive the remaining $45,000.

Who Are The Beneficiaries? 5

A question that comes up early on is who is entitled to the property of the decedent. To answer the question you first need to know how the property was titled (owned) as of the date of death.

There are three ways to own property. The decedent could have owned property jointly with another person; or in trust for another person; or the decedent could have owned property that was titled in his name only.

In general, upon the decedent's death:

Joint Property belongs to the surviving joint owner.

Trust Property belongs to the beneficiary of the Trust.

Property owned by the **decedent only** is inherited by the beneficiaries named in the Will.
If there is no Will, the property goes to his heirs according to the Rules Governing Intestate Succession.

NOTE ⇨ If the decedent was married, his spouse may have rights in his property.

This chapter describes each type of ownership in detail.

PROPERTY OWNED JOINTLY

Bank accounts, securities, motor vehicles, real property can all be owned jointly by two or more people. If one of the joint owners dies, then the survivor(s) continue to own their share of the property. Who owns the share belonging to the decedent depends on how the joint ownership was set up.

THE JOINT BANK ACCOUNT

When a bank account is opened the depositors sign an agreement with the bank that states the terms and conditions of the account. If the account is opened in two or more names, the contract will say whether each depositor has authority to make a withdrawal, or whether two signatures are necessary. The statement will also say whether there are rights of survivorship.

As explained in Chapter 4, unless the agreement with the bank states differently, it is presumed that the account is a Tenancy In Common. In such case, the surviving owner has no right to remove the decedent's share of the account. But if the account has rights of survivorship, the surviving owner is free to withdraw all of the monies from the account without the need to go through Probate. The surviving owner needs to keep in mind that Estateor Succession Taxes may be due on monies he inherits from the account. In addition, the Personal Representative has the right to ask him to contribute as much from the decedent's share of the account as is necessary to settle the decedent's Estate (Banking 675, Est. Powers & Trusts 2-1.1, 2-1.8, 12-1.2). If there are two surviving joint owners with rights of survivorship, either of them can go to the bank and withdraw all of the funds. It could become a race to the bank to take out all the money.

But would only serves to cause hard feelings. The remaining owners need to cooperate with each other and come to a joint decision about how to divide the account equitably. Each should withdraw his net contribution (what he contributed to the account, less what he withdrew) and half of the decedent's net contribution.

THE CONVENIENCE ACCOUNT

The decedent may have added someone to his bank or securities account for his own convenience and not with the intent of giving that person any right to the monies in the account. If that is the case, then the name on the account should reflect that intent, for example:

ALFRED RAY and MATHEW RAY
FOR THE CONVENIENCE OF ALFRED RAY

This is not a joint account. Should Alfred die, Mathew has no right to this account. The account becomes part of Alfred's estate. The account is the same as if it were held in Alfred's name only (Banking 678).

JOINTLY OWNED SECURITIES

You can determine whether the decedent owns a security alone or jointly with another by examining the face of the stock or bond certificate. If two names are printed on the certificate followed by a statement that the owners are Joint Tenants With Rights of Survivorship ("JTWRS"), the surviving owner can either cash in the security or ask the company to issue a new certificate in the name of the surviving owner. Each state has its own securities regulations. If a security held in two or more names, was registered or purchased in another state, and it does not indicate whether there are rights of survivorship, you need to contact the company to determine how the account was set up; i.e. with or without rights of survivorship.

If the decedent held his securities in a brokerage account, the name of the owner of that account is printed on the monthly or quarterly brokerage statement. Not all brokerage firms print the name of a joint owner on the brokerage statement, so you need to contact the firm to determine whether there is a surviving joint owner, or perhaps a beneficiary of the account. Request a copy of the contract that is the basis of the account. The contract will show when the account was opened and the terms of the account.

JOINTLY OWNED MOTOR VEHICLE

If a motor vehicle is held jointly, the name of each owner is printed on the title to the motor vehicle. In New York, if two names are on the title, either person has the right to transfer the car on his own signature. If one person dies, the other owns the car, 100%. You can change title to the car to your name only when the registration and/or car insurance expires.

It is important to change title as soon as you are able. You might be able to get a reduced insurance rate if there is only one person insured under the policy. Also, should the surviving owner be involved in an accident, and title has officially been changed, then there is no question that the Estate of the decedent is in any way liable for the accident.

Chapter 6 for an explanation of how to transfer title to the motor vehicle.

REAL PROPERTY OWNED JOINTLY

The name of the owner of real property is printed on the face of the deed. To determine whether the decedent owned the property jointly with another person, you need to look at the last recorded deed. The deed will indicate joint ownership. For example:

> This indenture, made this day, March 1, 2005, between ROBERT TRAYNOR, party of the first part, and SUSAN CODY and HENRY TRAYNOR, parties of the second part, as JOINT TENANTS
>
> . . .

Robert Traynor (party of the first part) is the **Grantor** of the deed. That means he transferred the property to Susan Cody and Henry Traynor (parties of the second part) who are the **Grantees** and present owners of the property. The deed states that Susan and Henry are JOINT TENANTS, meaning that they each have rights of survivorship. Should one of them die, the surviving joint tenant will own the property 100%. Nothing need be done to establish that ownership, however the decedent's name remains on the deed.

If you are the surviving joint owner of real property you may want to file the decedent's death certificate in the county where the property is located to let everyone know that you are now the sole owner of the property. See Chapter 6 for a discussion of the transfer of real property.

▤ DEED HELD AS TENANT IN COMMON

If a deed identifies the decedent and another as TENANTS IN COMMON, the decedent's share belongs to whomever the decedent named as his beneficiary in his Will. If he died without a Will, New York's Rules Governing Intestate Succession determine who inherits the decedent's share of the property. A Probate procedure will be necessary to transfer the decedent's share of the property to the proper beneficiary.

In New York, A deed must contain specific language indicating that the Grantees own the property as Joint Tenants, or that there are rights of survivorship, otherwise they own the property as Tenants In Common (Est. Powers & Trusts 6-2.2).

 **LAWYER**   THE AMBIGUOUS DEED

Most deeds clearly state whether there are rights of survivorship. But some deeds can be read two ways. For example, suppose a woman deeds her home to herself and her two children as follows:

> Ruth White, Grantor, ... to Ruth White jointly with Ralph White and Susan Peters.""

Did Ruth intend that they all be joint tenants? Or did she intend that if one of her children died first, that child's share would go to the deceased child's Estate? Best to consult with an attorney if you have any question about how to interpret the deed.

📄 AN ESTATE FOR LIFE

A *Life Estate* interest in real property means that the person who owns the Life Estate has the right to live in that property until he/she dies. You can identify a Life Estate interest by examining the face of the deed. If somewhere on the face of the deed you see the phrase

RESERVING A LIFE ESTATE

or

RESERVING AN ESTATE FOR LIFE

to the deceased Grantor, the Grantee now owns the property. For example, suppose the granting paragraph of the deed reads:

THIS INDENTURE, made this day, March 12, 2005
between ANN REILLY, party of the first part,
hereinafter referred to as "Grantor"
and, JAMES REILLY, party of the second part,
hereinafter referred to as "Grantee"

. . .

RESERVING A LIFE ESTATE TO THE GRANTOR

. . .

Ann is the owner of the Life Estate. James owns the *Remainder Interest* in the property. James has no right to occupy the property during Ann's lifetime, but once she dies, he will own the property 100%. He will be free to take possession of the property or transfer it, as he sees fit.

As with a Joint Tenancy, nothing need be done to establish his ownership of the property, however it is a good idea to have documents recorded to let people know that there is now just one owner. See Chapter 6 for a discussion of the transfer of real property.

▤ DEED HELD AS HUSBAND AND WIFE

If the decedent and his surviving spouse owned real property and the deed indicated that they were husband and wife; e.g. TODD AMES AND SUSAN AMES, HIS WIFE

or

TODD AMES AND SUSAN AMES, HUSBAND AND WIFE

or

TODD AMES AND SUSAN AMES, TENANTS BY ENTIRETY

then the surviving spouse now owns the property 100% (Est. Powers & Trusts 6-2.2).

THE COOPERATIVE APARTMENT CORPORATION

A Cooperative Apartment Corporation is a form of ownership of an apartment. Each apartment owner owns a share in the corporation and a lease to his apartment. If the decedent owned a Cooperative Apartment jointly with his spouse, then this is considered to be a Tenancy by the Entirety. If the decedent was not legally married, but the shares of stock and the lease identify them as being married, the property is owned as Joint Tenants, unless the documents specifically state that the ownership is a Tenancy In Common (Est. Powers & Trusts 6-2.1, 6-2.2).

 THERE COULD BE A LATER DEED

The discussion on the different types of ownership of real property assumes that you are in possession the most recent, valid deed. The decedent could have signed another, later deed. Before you come to a conclusion about who inherits the property it is advisable to have an attorney or a title insurance company conduct a title search to determine the owner of the property as of the decedent's date of death.

☎ LAWYER   THE OUT OF STATE DEED

The laws of the state or country where the property is located determine who inherits property in that state. If the decedent owned property in another state or country, then even if the decedent was a resident of New York, the laws of the state where the property is located determine who inherits property in that state (Est. Powers & Trusts 3-5.1 (b)(1)).

The laws of each state are similar, but not the same. Laws differ in how the deed needs to be worded in order to have a right of survivorship. Some states, like New York, a statement that the owners are Joint Tenants means that there are rights of survivorship. Other states, require the deed to actually state that there are rights of survivorship, otherwise, the property is considered to be a Tenancy In Common.

The rights of married couples varies significantly state to state. If the decedent was married, and owned property in his name only, his surviving spouse may have rights in that property. That is the case in Community Property states. In other states, a surviving spouse may have Dower rights or other statutory rights.

If the decedent owned property in another state, it is important to consult with an attorney in that state to determine who now owns the property.

BANK/ SECURITY ACCOUNTS
A bank account or security account that is registered in the name of the decedent "In Trust For" or "for the benefit of" someone will be turned over to the beneficiary once the financial institution has a certified copy of the death certificate. Sometimes the account is called a *Totten Trust* account.

BANK ACCOUNT HELD BY A TRUSTEE
If the bank or security account is registered in the name of the decedent "as Trustee under a Trust Agreement," that means the decedent was the Trustee of a Trust and the bank will turn over that account to the Successor Trustee of the Trust. Banks usually require a copy of the Trust Agreement or a Certificate that identifies the Successor Trustee, so the bank should be aware of his identity. If the Trust was amended to name a different Successor Trustee, you need to present the bank with a copy of that amendment together with a certified copy of the death certificate.

MOTOR VEHICLE
If the motor vehicle is held in the name of the decedent "as Trustee," then the motor vehicle continues to be Trust property. The Successor Trustee will need to contact the motor vehicle bureau to have title changed to that of the Successor Trustee. The Successor Trustee will then dispose of the car according to the terms of the Trust Agreement.

REAL PROPERTY

If the decedent had a Trust and put real property that he owned into the Trust, then the deed may read something like this:

> THIS INDENTURE made this day between
> JOHN ZAMORA and MARIA ZAMORA, his wife,
> parties of the first part. and
> JOHN ZAMORA, **Trustee of the**
> **JOHN ZAMORA REVOCABLE TRUST AGREEMENT**
> DATED MAY 2, 2005
> party of the second part,
> the real property described as
>
> . . .

The death of the Trustee of a Trust does not change the ownership of the property. It remains in the Trust. The Trust document might direct whoever takes John's place (the Successor Trustee) to sell or keep the property or perhaps give it to a beneficiary. If no instruction is given, the Successor Trustee will decide what to do with the property. If you are a beneficiary of the Trust and are concerned about what the Successor Trustee will do with the property, then consult with your attorney to learn about your rights under that Trust.

THE DEED OF TRUST

A Deed Of Trust is very different from the above described deed. The Deed of Trust is essentially a mortgage (Real Prop. 320). The owner of the property places title to the property with a Trustee as security for payment of monies owed to the lender. If the debt is not paid, the Trustee (after proper foreclosure on the property) will deliver title to the property to the beneficiary of the Deed of Trust, namely the lender.

PROPERTY IN DECEDENT'S NAME ONLY

If the decedent owned property that was in his name only (not jointly or in trust for someone), then some sort of Probate procedure will be necessary before the heirs can get possession of that property. Who is entitled to the decedent's Probate Estate depends on whether the decedent died with or without a Will. If the decedent died *testate* (with a Will), then the beneficiaries of the decedent's property are identified in the Will.

If the decedent died without a Will, then New York's Rules Governing Intestate Succession determine who inherits the decedent's Probate Estate and what percentage of the Probate Estate each heir is to receive, once all the bills and costs of administering the Probate procedure are paid.

The law recognizes the right of the family to inherit the decedent's property. The law covers all possible relationships beginning with the decedent's spouse. But before we discuss the rights of the surviving spouse, we need to consider whether decedent had a marriage that is considered as being valid within state of New York.

BEING MARRIED IN NEW YORK

Under New York law, a marriage is a civil contract entered into voluntarily by the parties (Dom. Rel. 10). To be married in New York means that a man and a woman have obtained a marriage license from the town or city clerk and then solemnized the marriage by a state or religious ceremony. Parental consent to marry is required for anyone under 18. Court permission is required if the child is under 16, however marriage under the age of 14 is prohibited (Dom. Rel. 11, 13, 15, 15-a).

There are certain unions that are specifically banned within New York:

☒   No license can be granted if either party is currently married to another person (Dom. Rel 6).

New York law does not bar marriages between cousins, however the law prohibits the marriage of those:

☒   who are ancestors (parent, grandparents, etc.)
     or descendants (child, grandchild, etc.)
     of each other
☒   who are aunt and nephew or uncle and niece
☒   who are brother and sister. This includes siblings
     who are half blood; i.e. they have only one parent
     in common (Dom. Rel. 5).

THE COMMON LAW MARRIAGE

A Common Law marriage is one that has not been solemnized by ceremony. It is more than just living together. The couple must agree to live together as man and wife, and then publicly hold themselves out as being married; i.e., tell friends, family and business acquaintances, that they are married. Many states no longer recognize a Common Law marriage as being valid, and have passed laws to that effect. The state of New York does not recognize a Common Law marriage that was entered into in the state of New York after April 29, 1933 (*Matter of Benjamin*, 34 N.Y.2d 27).

New York respects the laws of other states. Courts have ruled that they will recognize a Common Law marriage as being valid in New York if it was valid in the state where the couple entered into the marriage (*Mott v. Duncan Petroleum*, 414 N.E.2d 657). It is important to consult with an attorney if you have any question about the validity of the decedent's marriage.

SAME SEX MARRIAGES

Vermont was the first state to recognize a same sex marriage, which they refer to as a "civil union." Several other states have passed statutes, specifically denying marital status to couples of the same gender. Some states have passed laws giving certain rights to same sex partners within that state. For example, California has passed laws giving registered *Domestic Partners* the same rights as those of married partners within that state. Hawaii offers similar rights to couples registered as *Reciprocal Beneficiaries* within their state. In New Jersey, couples of the same gender can register as Domestic Partners with the New Jersey State Registrar. Once registered, they are afforded certain limited rights such as the right to visit a hospitalized Domestic Partner and to make medical decisions for their incapacitated Partner.

New York recognizes a Domestic Partner relationship that was entered into in another state for purposes of health care visitation rights (Pub. Health 2805-q). Employers, (including state employers), may maintain a Domestic Partner registry (Work. Comp. 4). However as of the year 2005, New York does not have a state wide registration system. However, there have been several cases involving same sex unions. In *Levin v Yeshiva University*, 96 N.Y. 2d 484 (2001), the court quoted the New York City Administrative Code Section 8-107(5)(a)(1) which makes it unlawful " . . . to refuse housing accommodations because of that persons 'actual or perceived race, creed, color, national origin, gender, age, disability, <u>sexual orientation</u>, marital status, ... ' "

In Raum v. Restaurant Associates, Inc., 252 A.D.2d 369 (1st Dept 1998), the court upheld the right of a homosexual partner to bring a wrongful death action as authorized by Est. Powers & Trusts 5-4.1. (See page 19 for a discussion of a wrongful death action).

Yet, New York courts have ruled that the surviving partner of a homosexual union is not considered to be a surviving spouse for purposes of New York's laws relating to Estates, Powers and Trusts (*Matter of Cooper*, 187 A.D.2d 128 (2d Dept. 1993)), so, for the purposes of Intestate Succession, a Domestic Partner in New York has no rights of inheritance.

DISQUALIFYING THE SURVIVING SPOUSE

It is not necessary to prove to the court that the surviving spouse and the decedent had a valid marriage, however, the surviving spouse can be disqualified from inheriting property under New York's Rules Governing Intestate Succession if any of the following are brought to the attention of the court:

☒ The surviving spouse obtained a divorce or annulment in this or any other state (Dom. Rel 6).

☒ Their relationship was incestuous; i.e., they were related as prohibited by New York statute (Dom. Rel. 5) (see page 119).

☒ A final decree or judgment of separation was in effect as of the date of death.

☒ The surviving spouse abandoned the decedent, and that abandonment continued until his death.

☒ The surviving spouse failed or refused to provide support even though he had the means and the duty to do so — unless he resumed and continued such support until the death (Est. Powers & Trusts 5-1.2).

If the decedent died without a Will, the state of New York provides one for him in the form of its *Rules Governing Intestate Succession*. Once his debts, funeral expenses, and the cost of the Probate is paid, whatever is left (his net Probate Estate) is distributed as follows:

✧ DESCENDANT, NO SPOUSE ✧

If the decedent was single and had *lineal descendants* (children, grandchildren, great-grandchildren, etc.), they inherit all of his property *by representation*. New York statute (Est. Powers & Trusts 1-2.16) defines the term "by representation" as follows:

> By representation means a disposition or distribution of property made in the following manner to persons who take as issue of a deceased ancestor:
>
> The property so passing is divided into as many equal shares as there are (i) surviving issue in the generation nearest to the deceased ancestor which contains one or more surviving issue and (ii) deceased issue in the same generation who left surviving issue, if any. Each surviving member in such nearest generation is allocated one share. The remaining shares, if any, are combined and then divided in the same manner among the surviving issue who are allocated a share had pre-deceased the decedent without issue.

If you understood the above definition and you are not a lawyer, you missed your calling. For the rest of us (even lawyers) its a head-scratcher. Perhaps the best way to explain the term is through example:

ALL CHILDREN SURVIVE
Suppose the decedent was unmarried with 4 children, Ann, Barry, Carl, David and he dies intestate, then each of his children get 25% of his estate.

CHILD WITHOUT DESCENDANTS DIES BEFORE DECEDENT

If Ann dies before her father leaving no descendants, Barry, Carl and David divide the estate between them. Each gets one third.

CHILDREN WITH DESCENDANTS DIES BEFORE DECEDENT

Suppose instead that only Carl and David survived their father. If Ann died leaving 2 children and Barry died leaving 3 children, the Estate is divided into 4 shares — one for each surviving child and one share for each deceased child who left descendants. Carl and David each get their share, namely Carl gets 25% of the Estate and David gets 25%. The remaining shares are combined and then divided equally among the five grandchildren, with each grand-child getting 10% of the Estate.

✧ MARRIED WITH DESCENDANT ✧

If the decedent was married, his spouse is entitled to $50,000 plus half of whatever is left of his Probate Estate after all the bills and expenses are paid. The decedent's children get the other half, by representation (Est. Powers & Trusts 4-1.1 (a)(1)).

✧ MARRIED WITHOUT DESCENDANT ✧

The surviving spouse is entitled to the entire Probate Estate if the decedent died and was not survived by a descendant (Est. Powers & Trusts 4-1.1 (a)(2)).

✧ SINGLE, NO DESCENDANT ✧

The Probate Estate of a single decedent, who has no descendants, is divided equally between his parents. If only one of the decedent's parents is alive, all of the property goes to that parent. If neither parent is alive, the Estate goes to the decedent's brothers and sisters, by representation.

HALF BLOOD INHERITS THE SAME AS WHOLE BLOOD

A person related to the decedent by half blood, is entitled to inherit the same as if he were of whole blood (Est. Powers & Trusts 4-1.1 (5) and (7b)). For example, if the decedent was survived by a brother with the same set of parents and a brother with the same father and a different mother, the two brothers are each entitled to the same share of the Estate.

If the decedent had no brothers, sisters, nephews or nieces, his Estate is divided in half with half going to his surviving maternal grandparents and the other half going to his surviving paternal grandparents. If neither maternal grandparent survives the decedent, the share goes to their descendants, by representation. If neither paternal grandparent survives the decedent, the share goes to their descendants by representation.

New York statute (Estates 4-1.1 (6) and (7)) makes a distinction about the way the grandparent's share is distributed if the grandparent is not survived by someone closer than a grandchild. The order of distribution is fairly complex, so if a relation inherits at this level it is best to consult with an attorney before you decide who is entitled to the decedent's intestate property.

✧ THE STATE: HEIR OF LAST RESORT

If a person dies without a Will and he has absolutely no relations, his property goes to the state of New York. The property is considered to be abandoned property and is regulated by the New York's abandoned property law (Est. Powers & Trusts 4-1.5).

THE RIGHTS OF A CHILD

THE NON-MARITAL CHILD

A child born out of wedlock has the same right to inherit from his/her natural father as does one born in wedlock, provided any one of the following are true:

☑ He married the mother after the birth.

☑ He acknowledged the child as his own by signing and filing a legal document with the New York Department of Social Services.

☑ His paternity was established by clear and convincing evidence and he openly treated the child as his own (Dom. Rel. 24, Est. Power & Trusts 4-1.2).

If the decedent denied he was the child's father, it will take a Court procedure to establish (or disprove) paternity.

THE ADOPTED CHILD

An adopted person has the same right to inherit property under the Rules Governing Intestate Success from his adoptive parents as does a natural child. The adopted child has no right to inherit from his natural parents, with the exception of the natural parent who is married to the adoptive parent. For example, should a child be adopted by his stepfather, the child has the right to inherit from his stepfather and all of the stepfather's relatives and also from his mother and all of his maternal relatives (Dom. Rel. 117, Est. Powers & Trusts 1-2.10).

THE AFTERBORN CHILD

A child who was conceived prior to the decedent's death, and born to the surviving spouse after the death, has the same right to inherit as any other natural child of the decedent (Est. Powers & Trusts 2-1.3, 4-1.1 (c)).

NO SHARE FOR NEGLECTFUL PARENT

A parent who willfully abandoned the care and support of his/her child while the child was under 21, is not entitled to inherit from the child under New York's Rules Governing Intestate Succession, unless he later resumed his parental relationship and duties and continued with that relationship until the death of the child. If the parent did not resume the care, the child's Estate is distributed as if the parent died before the child (Est. Powers & Trusts 4-1.4).

Special Situation

NO SHARE FOR KILLER

Under New York law anyone who is found guilty of the murder of the decedent in first or second degree can be barred from profiting from the crime. If a trial is in progress for the murder, any joint account owned by the decedent and the accused, can be frozen by the court, pending the outcome of the trial (Est. Powers & Trusts 4-1.6).

Even if the accused is not found criminally liable, the family can sue him for the wrongful death of the decedent. Depending on the nature of the injury, the court may award punitive damages to the decedent's Estate. The court will decide how the money is to be distributed. The court will award the greater amount to those who have suffered most from the loss. If the person who committed the act was a beneficiary of the estate, the share he would have received can be used to satisfy the judgment (Est. Powers & Trusts 5-4.1, 5-4.3).

WHO DIED FIRST?

Sometimes it happens that two family members die simultaneously, and no one knows who died first. For example, suppose a husband and wife die together in a car crash, how is the property distributed in that case?

New York statute (Est. Powers & Trusts 2-1.6) provides for an orderly distribution of their respective Estates.

PROCEEDS OF A LIFE INSURANCE POLICY

Suppose the husband is insured, with his wife as the beneficiary of his life insurance policy. The proceeds of the policy will be distributed as if the wife died before her husband. The proceeds will be given to the alternate beneficiary named in the policy. If no alternate beneficiary was named, the proceeds of the policy will go to the insured party (in this case, the husband).

JOINTLY OWNED PROPERTY

Property owned jointly by the couple, with no provision for who is to inherit the property should they both die, is divided with half going to the Estate of the husband and the other half to the Estate of the wife. If they each have a Will, the husband's half is distributed according to his Will and the wife's half according to her Will. If they die without a Will, then each half is distributed according to New York's Rules Governing Intestate Succession.

WHEN TO CHALLENGE THE WILL

It is not uncommon for a family member to be unhappy with the way the decedent willed his property. If you are tempted to challenge a Will, first consider whether the Will is valid under New York law. In New York, a Will is presumed valid if at the time the decedent made the Will if he was 18 years of age or older and of sound mind and memory (Est. Powers & Trusts 3-1.1).

New York Courts have ruled that a person is considered to be of sound mind and memory if at the time he signed the Will, he knew:

➢ what property he owned AND

➢ what he was doing (namely making a Will) AND

➢ who would, under ordinary circumstances, expect to inherit his property AND

➢ his relationship with those who expected to inherit his property
(*Matter of Kumstar*, 487 N.E. 2d 271 (NY 1985)).

The first step in the Probate procedure is to have the Probate court determine whether the Will presented is valid. There should be no problem having the Will accepted into Probate, if the Will is in writing and signed by the Will maker in the presence of at least two credible witnesses. But suppose the decedent wrote out a Will in his own hand and signed it with no one present?

☒ THE UNWITNESSED WILL

A Will written in the Will maker's hand is called a **holographic Will**. The state of New York does not recognize such a Will as being valid unless the Will was written by a member of the armed forces while he was in combat. Once the soldier returns from battle he must write one in conformity with New York law because the holographic Will is not accepted as valid if it has been more than a year since the soldier returned from battle.

Similarly, a mariner at sea may make a holographic Will, but that Will can only be accepted into Probate if he dies within three years of writing it (Est. Powers & Trusts 3-2.2).

The problem with a holographic Will is its authenticity. Because no one saw the decedent sign the Will, it is hard to determine whether itl was written by the decedent or is a forgery. If all the decedent left was a holographic Will, you should consult with an attorney experienced in Probate matters.

☒ THE WILL WITNESSED BY A BENEFICIARY

Neither of the witnesses of the decedent's Will should be a beneficiary of the Will. Under New York law any gift made in a Will to someone who witnessed the Will cannot be given to that witness unless there are at least two other witnesses to the Will who are not beneficiaries under the Will. The Will is not invalid because a beneficiary of the Will, witnessed the Will. It just means that the beneficiary is not entitled to receive the gift made in the Will. The gift will become part of the **Residuary Estate**, i.e., what is left once all expenses are paid and all specific gifts are made.

If the beneficiary witness is entitled to an inheritance according to the Rules Governing Intestate Succession, he can inherit as much of the Residuary Estate as he would have received had the Will maker died without a Will (Est. Powers & Trusts 3-3.2).

☒ UNDUE INFLUENCE

The reason New York law discourages a beneficiary of the Will to be a witness to the Will is that of **undue influence**. Undue influence occurs whenever someone exerts such pressure on the Will maker so that he is not acting according to his own free will. But if the Will is properly signed and witnessed, according to New York law, undue influence is not easily proven. Courts have ruled that it is necessary to examine all the facts and circumstances of the case to determine whether the Will maker was dependent upon and subject to the control of the person who supposedly wielded such influence (*Matter of Kumstar*, 487 N.E.2d 271 (NY, 1985)).

☒   THE VERBAL WILL

Picture a death bed scene. The elderly gentleman is surrounded by several family members. In a whisper, just audible enough to be heard, he says: "Even though I am a wealthy man, I never got around to making a Will. You all have been good to me, but I did want my entire fortune to go to my nephew, Robert. He has been like a son to me. "

Do you think Robert can inherit his Uncle's Estate?

Not in New York unless:

⇨   Someone writes down his uncles's wishes, AND

⇨   The uncle acknowledges that this is his Will, AND

⇨   The uncle signs the Will, or at his request has someone sign it for him, AND

⇨   Two other people sign the Will as witnesses (Est. Powers & Trusts 3-2.1).

Considering that the uncle's relatives will probably inherit the fortune under New York's Rules Governing Intestate Succession, it is doubtful that Robert is in danger of becoming wealthy at any time in the near future.

Sometimes a person who is of sound mind, makes a Will, but that Will has the effect of giving a spouse or a minor child less than is required to receive under New York law. One such example is that of Nancy. Hers was not an easy life. She divorced her hard drinking first husband. The final judgment gave her their homestead, some securities and sole custody of their daughter, Anne. After the divorce, Nancy had her attorney prepare a Will leaving all she owned to Anne. She had the attorney change the deed to her name and Anne, as joint tenants.

Some years later Nancy met and married Harry. He moved into her home and they later had twin boys. Nancy never did get around to changing the Will once she remarried.

Anne was 18, and her half-brothers 12, when Nancy died after a lengthy battle with cancer. Just before she died, Nancy gave Anne $10,000 because she wanted to be sure Anne had enough cash for her first semester of college.

Nancy did not have much when she died — the house, now worth $80,000, her furnishings, her car (worth $12,000) and securities and bank accounts worth about $40,000.

When the funeral was over, Harry discovered the Will (leaving all to Anne). He also found the cancelled $10,000 check, but the thing that sent him ballistic, was having Anne tell him that she was putting the house up for sale.

" I was a good husband to Nancy, supporting and taking care of her all during her illness. It was me, and not her daughter, who was at her side when she died. Don't I have Dower Rights or something? "

"Dower rights are for wives. Curtesy rights are for husbands, but those were abolished here in New York back in 1930. However, you are entitled to an *Elective Share* of her Estate unless you *waived* (gave up) those rights by signing a prenuptial or postnuptial agreement (Real Prop. 189, 190, Est. Powers & Trusts 5-1.1-A). "

"No. I never signed anything."

"In that case, New York law gives you the right to $50,000 or one third of your wife's *net estate* whichever is the greater value. The net estate consists of all of the property your wife owned including the homestead that she held jointly with Anne and the $10,000 she gave to her daughter in contemplation of her death. In addition, you are entitled to keep all of the household furnishing (up to $10,000 in value), money or other personal property (up to $15,000) and your wife's car (Est. Powers & Trusts 5-3.1)."

"Sounds good to me. And what about my sons. Do they have any rights?"

"They sure do. New York law provides that if a child is born after a Will is made, that child is entitled to inherit as much as his siblings. This means that whatever Anne inherits will be split three ways, with all three children getting an equal share (Est. Powers & Trusts 5-3.2)."

No doubt Nancy did not think that her Will would be challenged, but challenged it was. By the time the funeral expenses, medical bills, and the cost of probating the Estate were paid, there was little left for Anne.

Had Nancy known about New York law, she could have consulted with an attorney and set up an Estate plan that would have accomplished her goals. But, the moral of the story, for the purpose of this discussion, is that if you believe that the decedent's Will is not valid or is not drafted according to New York law, you need to consult with an attorney experienced in Probate matters to determine your legal rights under that Will.

Getting Possession Of The Property 6

Knowing who is entitled to receive the decedent's property is one thing. Getting that property is another. As explained in the previous chapter, if the decedent held property jointly with someone, or in a Trust for someone, the property now belongs to the joint owner or beneficiary. If it is personal property such as a bank account or a security, the beneficiary can usually get possession of the property by giving a certified copy of the death certificate to the financial institution.

If the decedent had real or personal property in his name only, or if he held property as a Tenant In Common, then some sort of Probate proceeding may be necessary in order to transfer ownership to the proper beneficiary. The assistance of an attorney may be required should a full Probate proceeding be necessary, but there are many items that can be transferred without legal assistance. This chapter explains how to get possession of those items.

The chapter also contains an explanation of the different kinds of Probate procedures and when it is appropriate to use that procedure.

Too often, the first person to discover the body will help himself to the decedent's **personal effects** (clothing, jewelry, appliances, electrical equipment, cameras, books, stamp or coin collection, household items and furnishing, etc.). Unless that person is the decedent's sole beneficiary, such action is unconscionable, if not illegal.

As explained in Chapter 4, if the decedent was married, as of the date of death, certain of his personal property belongs to his surviving spouse (Est. Powers & Trusts 5-3.1). That includes all of his household furniture and furnishings (up to $10,000 in value), the family bible, family pictures, video tapes, computer discs, software and books (up to $1,000 in value), etc. See page 100 for a complete list of items that become the property of the surviving spouse. In the absence of a surviving spouse, the property belongs to his children who are under the age of 21 (Est. Powers & Trusts 5-3.1).

The Personal Representative has the duty to distribute the rest of his personal property as directed in the decedent's Will, or if no Will, according the Rules Governing Intestate Succession. If Probate is not necessary, the decedent's next of kin, as determined by the Rules Governing Intestate Succession, need to divide all of the personal effects among themselves in approximately equal proportions.

What's Equal?
The decedent's Will may direct that the decedent's personal property be divided equally between two or more beneficiaries. The problem with the term "equal" is that people have different ideas of what "equal" means.

Unless there is clear evidence that the decedent's Will meant something else, "equal" refers to the monetary value of the item and not to the number of items received. For example, to divide the decedent's personal effects equally, one beneficiary may receive an expensive item of jewelry and another beneficiary may receive several items whose overall value is approximately equal to that single piece of jewelry.

When distributing personal effects there needs to be cooperation and perhaps compromise, or else bitter arguments might arise over items of little monetary value. One such argument occurred when an elderly woman died who was rich only in her love for her five children and ten grandchildren. After the funeral, the children gathered in their mother's apartment. Each child had his/her own furnishings and no need for anything in the apartment. They agreed to donate all of their mother's personal effects to a local charity with the exception of a few items of sentimental value.

Each child took some small item as a remembrance — a handkerchief, a large platter that their mother used to serve family dinners, a doily their mother crocheted. Things went smoothly until it came to her photograph album. Frank, the youngest sibling, said, "I'll take this." Marie objected saying "But there are pictures in that album that I want."

Frank retorted, "You already took all the pictures Mom had on her dresser."

The argument went downhill from there. Unsettled sibling rivalries boiled over, fueled by the hurt of the loss that they were all experiencing.

It almost came to blows when the eldest settled the argument. "Frank you make copies of all of the photos in the album for Marie. Marie, you make copies of all of the pictures that you took and give them to Frank. This way you both will have a complete set of Mom's pictures. And while you're at it, make copies for the rest of us."

NON-PROBATE TRANSFERS

A *Non-probate transfer* is a transfer of the decedent's property without the need for Probate. For example, if the decedent owned a bank account jointly with another with rights of survivorship, or if he had a bank account in his name only "In Trust For" someone, all the beneficiary need do is produce a death certificate and proper identification, and the bank will turn over the property to him. However, as explained in Chapter 4, the decedent's share of a joint account may be needed to pay taxes or settle the decedent's Estate; and all of the "In Trust For" account is available to pay taxes and settle the decedent's Estate (Est. Powers & Trusts 2-1.1, 2-1.8, 7-5.5, 12-1.2).

As previously explained, a car that is owned jointly becomes the property of the surviving joint owner. The surviving owner can go to the nearest Department of Motor Vehicles and transfer the car to his name only. He can do this on his signature alone, provided there is no lien on the car. If monies are owed on the car, title to the car cannot be changed until the lien is released.

Before going to the DMV, you might want to call them to determine the cost of the transfer and what documents they require: Upstate New York: (800) 225-5368
From 516, 631 and 914 area codes: (800) 342-5368
Metropolitan New York: (212) 645-5550 or (718) 966-6155
For the hearing impaired: within state TDD (800) 368-1186

It is relatively simple to transfer the decedent's motor vehicle. If the value does not exceed $15,000 and the decedent is survived by a spouse or child under 21, the spouse, child (or Guardian of the child) can make the transfer by signing an *Affidavit* (a sworn statement that the facts are true) in the presence of a notary public stating that:

☑ The spouse (or child) is the proper successor to the motor vehicle

☑ The motor vehicle does not exceed $15,000 in value

☑ The motor vehicle is the only vehicle being transferred according to Estates 5-3.1.

The Department of Motor Vehicles provides the Affidavit (Form MV-349.1)

If there is no Will, spouse, or child under 21, and Probate is not necessary, the next of kin can use form MV-349 to transfer title to the motor vehicle. The form contains an Affidavit by the person taking possession of the car. Other members of the decedent's immediate family may need to consent to the transfer by signing the back of the form.

TRANSFER IF VALID WILL

If a Probate proceeding is necessary, then regardless of its value, it is up to the Personal Representative to transfer the car to the proper beneficiary. The surviving spouse has the right to the decedent's car as Exempt Property. If the spouse does not want the car, or if the decedent was single, the Personal Representative will transfer the car according to the terms of the Will.

If the Will makes a *specific gift* of the car, the Personal Representative will transfer the car to that person. If there was no mention of the car in the decedent's Will, it goes to the **residuary beneficiaries** under the Will, i.e., those who inherit whatever is left once all the bills have been paid and all the special gifts made in the Will are distributed. If the decedent did not have a Will, the car goes to the decedent's next of kin as determined by New York's Rules Governing Intestate Succession.

TRANSFER WHEN MORE THAN ONE BENEFICIARY

If there is more than one person with the right to inherit the car, then they all can take title to the car. That may not be a practical thing to do since only one person can drive the car at any given time and if one gets into an accident, then they all can be held liable. The better route is for the beneficiaries to agree to have one person take title. That beneficiary will need to compensate the others for their share of the car. In such case, the beneficiaries need to come to an agreement as to the value of the car.

DETERMINING THE VALUE OF THE CAR

Cars are valued in different ways. The *collateral* value of the car is the value that banks use to evaluate the car for purposes of making a loan to the owner of the car. If you were to trade in a car for the purpose of purchasing a new one, the car dealer would offer you its *wholesale* value. Were you to purchase that same car from a car dealer, he would price it at its *retail* or *fair market value*. Usually the retail price is highest, wholesale is lowest and its collateral value is somewhere in between.

You can call your local bank to get the collateral value of the car. It may be more difficult to obtain the wholesale value because the amount of money a dealer is willing to pay depends on the value of the new car that you are purchasing. You can determine the car's retail value by looking at comparable used car advertisements in the local newspaper.

Rather than going through the effort of determining these three values, you can use your Internet search engine to look up the Kelly Blue Book Value. This publication gives Low, Average and High Blue Book Values which correspond to the wholesale, collateral and retail values.

Once the fair market value of the car is determined, the beneficiary who takes the car will be considered to have received that value as part of his inheritance. If none of the beneficiaries want the car, the Personal Representative will sell it and add the proceeds to the amount distributed to the beneficiaries.

It is a good idea to limit the use of the car until it is sold or transferred to the beneficiary. If the decedent's car is involved in an accident before the car is transferred to the new owner, the decedent's Estate may be liable for the damage. Having adequate insurance on the car may save the Estate from monetary loss, but a pending lawsuit could delay Probate and prevent any money from being distributed to the beneficiaries until the lawsuit is settled.

The leased car is not an asset of the Estate because the decedent did not own the car. The leased car is a liability to the Estate because the decedent was obligated to pay the balance of the monies owed on the lease agreement. The Personal Representative, or next of kin, need to work out an agreement with the company to either assign the lease to a beneficiary or family member who will agree to pay for the lease — or to have the Estate pay off the lease by purchasing the car under the terms of the lease agreement.

Some lenders will allow the lease to be assigned to a beneficiary provided the Estate remains liable for the balance of payment. In such cases, it is better to have the beneficiary refinance the car and have the original lease agreement paid in full.

If the remaining payments exceed the current market value of the car, there may be a temptation to hand the keys over to the leasing company. This may not be the best strategy, because the leasing company can sell the car and then sue the Estate for the balance of the monies owed. If the decedent had no assets or if the only assets he had are creditor proof, then simply returning the car may be an option. But if the decedent's Estate has assets available to pay the balance of the lease payments, the Personal Representative needs to arrange to have the car transferred in a way that releases the Estate from all further liability.

TRANSFERRING THE MOBILE HOME

A mobile home is transferred the same as any other motor vehicle. Before transferring the motor vehicle, you need to find out whether the land on which the mobile home is located was leased or owned by the decedent. If the decedent was renting space in a trailer park, then you need to contact the trailer park owner to transfer the lease agreement to the beneficiary of the mobile home. If the decedent owned the land under the mobile home, a Probate proceeding will be necessary to transfer the land to the proper beneficiary. Transferring real property is discussed later in this chapter.

TRANSFERRING WATERCRAFT & ALL-TERRAIN VEHICLES

The New York State Department of Motor Vehicles is in charge of the title and registration of motor vehicles, including motorized scooters and bicycles, boats 14' in length or greater, and all-terrains vehicles ("ATV").

They do not register snowmobiles and off-highway motorcycles (Veh. & Traf. 2102). If the beneficiary of a motorcycle does not use his motorcycle on public roadways, he does not need to register it with the Department of Motor Vehicles.

TRANSFERRING AIRCRAFT

As explained in Chapter 3, the Civil Aviation Registry of the Federal Aviation Administration ("FAA") is in charge of the ownership and security documents filed with the FAA. You will need to contact them at (405) 954-3116 for information about how to transfer title to the proper beneficiary. The New York Department of Transportation is in charge of Aviation Services, however they do not require state registration for aircraft or pilots.

See their Web site for information about Aviation Services.

 NYS DEPARTMENT OF TRANSPORTATION
http://www.dot.state.ny.us

If the aircraft is being sold, a NYS Sales Tax will need to be paid within twenty (20) days of delivery. Sales tax form ST130 will need to be filed with the NYS Department of Taxation and Finance.

You can call them at (800) 462-8100 to get a copy of form ST130 or you can download the form from their Web site. http://www.tax.state.ny.us.

THE FEDERAL INCOME TAX REFUND

Any refund due to the decedent under a joint federal income tax return filed by his surviving spouse will be sent to the surviving spouse. If the decedent's Personal Representative filed the final return, then the refund check will be sent to him to be deposited to the Estate account.

If the decedent was single and no Probate proceeding is necessary, then whoever is entitled to the decedent's Estate is entitled to the refund check. If you are the beneficiary of the decedent's Estate, you can obtain the refund by filing IRS form 1310 along with the decedent's final income tax return (the 1040). You can obtain form 1310 from the decedent's accountant, or if he did not have an accountant and you wish to file yourself, you can call the IRS at (800) 829-3676 to obtain the form.

You can download instructions, publications and forms from the Internal Revenue Service by going to the **FORMS AND PUBLICATIONS** section of their Web site.

 INTERNAL REVENUE SERVICE
http://www.irs.gov/

The Personal Representative does not need to file form 1310 because once he files the decedent's final income tax return, any refund will be forwarded to him. Similarly, it is not necessary for the surviving spouse who filed a joint return to file form 1310.

THE STATE INCOME TAX REFUND

The decedent's final New York income tax return needs to be filed at the same time the federal income tax return is filed (Tax Law 651). If the decedent was married, his surviving spouse can file a joint return. If Probate is necessary, the Personal Representative has the responsibility of filing the final tax return.

If Probate is not necessary, the next of kin can file the final return. If there is a refund due, the next of kin will need to complete a Survivor's Affidavit Form (AU 217). You can get the form from your accountant or you can call (800) 225-5829.

You can also obtain the form from the New York State Income Tax Web site: http://www.tax.state.ny.us

DEPOSITING THE TAX REFUND

If the decedent was not married, and the Personal Representative filed the final return, the refund check will be sent to him to be deposited into the Estate account. If no Probate proceeding is necessary and the refund check (or any other check) is in the name of the decedent, you can deposit it into the decedent's bank account. You can get the money in the decedent's account by using whatever Probate procedure is appropriate.

Depending on the amount in the account, you may be able to get the funds by means of an Affidavit as explained on the next page.

TRANSFERRING PROPERTY BY AFFIDAVIT

New York statute (Surr. Ct. Proc. Act 1310) was designed to transfer certain personal property to the family of the decedent quickly and without the need for Probate. Items that can be transferred under this statute are those items belonging to the decedent only, or to his Estate, including:

- ✧ the decedent's last pay check
- ✧ the decedent's bank or securities account
- ✧ any of his personal property deposited with the medical examiner, nursing home, hospital, or similar agency
- ✧ any insurance benefit, pension or annuity payable to the decedent's estate

The amount that can be transferred, and when it can be transferred, depends on who is to receive the property:

- ➪ Anytime after the death, up to $30,000, to the spouse.
- ➪ At least 30 days after the death, up to $15,000 to the decedent's adult child, or parent, or brother or sister, or niece or nephew
- ➪ At least six months after the death, up to $5,000 to anyone entitled to the property either by Will or intestate succession, or to someone who paid for the decedent's funeral expenses.

The spouse can get the property by submitting a certified copy of the death certificate and signing an Affidavit that states that all of the property that the spouse is receiving by means of Affidavit does not exceed $30,000. If the property is to go to a family member, the family member can get the property by signing an Affidavit in the form described on the next page.

AFFIDAVIT FOR TRANSFER OF PERSONAL PROPERTY
pursuant to Surrogate's Court Procedure 1310 (3)

Affiant declares that the following is true:

1. The decedent_____ (name)
died on_____ (date) at the county of _____
state of _____.

2. At least 30 days have elapsed since the date of death as shown in the certified copy of the death certificate of the decedent which is attached to this affidavit.

3. No fiduciary has qualified or been appointed to administer the decedent's estate.

4. The relationship of the affiant to the decedent is _____

5. The names and addresses of the persons entitled to and who will receive the money paid:_____
_____.

6. The following is a description of the property of the decedent that is to be paid, transferred, or delivered to those identified in paragraph 5:
_____

7. After diligent inquiry, Affiant states that this payment and all other payments made pursuant to Surrogate's Court Procedure 1310 (3) do not exceed $15,000.

I affirm or declare, under penalty of perjury under the laws of the State of New York, that the foregoing is true and correct.

Affiant Name _____
Affiant Signature _____ date_____
Affiant address:_____

Signed at _____ County, state of _____
_____
Notary Signature and Seal

The Affidavit is appropriate to use if all the decedent left was a few thousand dollars, no debts to speak of, and all of his Estate goes to one or two people. But suppose the decedent left a small amount of money and it goes to several people, or perhaps several of the decedent's creditors need to be paid. In that case, someone needs to take responsibility to settle the Estate and then distribute whatever is left to the proper beneficiary. There is a relatively simple Probate procedure designed to handle such situations. It is called a *Summary Procedure*.

To qualify for a Summary Procedure, the total amount of personal property to be transferred must not exceed $20,000, not counting all of the things that are exempt for the benefit of the family (see page 100). Someone needs to be appointed as *Voluntary Administrator* to settle the Estate. If the decedent had a Will, the person he named as Executor is entitled to be appointed. If the decedent died without a valid Will, the spouse has top priority for the appointment. If there is no spouse, or the spouse declines to serve, an adult child or grandchild can serve as Voluntary Administrator. If none of these, the decedent's parent, brother or sister, niece or nephew, aunt or uncle, in that order, can serve.

The position of Voluntary Administrator is one of trust. Whoever takes on the job does so without pay and without bond. Once the family agrees as to who is to serve as Voluntary Administrator, that person needs to go to the Surrogate's Court in the county of the decedent's residence in order to be appointed. If the decedent was not a resident of the state, then to the Surrogate's Court in the county where the personal property is located (Surr. Ct. Proc. Act 1301, 1302, 1303, 1304).

If you are going to be Voluntary Administrator, you may save time by first calling the Clerk and asking:

How do I get to the courthouse?
When is the best time to meet with the Clerk?
What documents or information should I bring?
How much money will it cost?

You will need to sign an Affidavit given to you by the Clerk. If someone has a higher priority to be appointed as Voluntary Administrator, that person will need to agree, in writing, to your appointment. The Clerk will send out a post card telling those who have the right to inherit the decedent's property, that you have started a Summary procedure.

Once the Clerk is satisfied that the Estate qualifies for the Summary Administration, he will give you a document called a **Short Certificate**. With the Short Certificate you will be able to get possession of the decedent's property. You will need to deposit all of the money you collect into a bank account that you open as Voluntary Administrator. You will pay all of the decedent's bills from this account, signing your name as Voluntary Administrator on all the checks. You will distribute whatever is left to the proper beneficiary (Surr. Ct. Proc. Act 1307, 1308).

It is important that you do all this in an honest and conscientious manner, else the decedent's creditors and beneficiaries have the right to seek reimbursement from you for any error or wrongdoing.

Once you distribute the money, you need to report back to the Clerk with a full accounting of how much money you collected and to whom it was given.

GETTING THE CONTENTS OF THE SAFE DEPOSIT BOX

If the decedent leased a safe deposit box together with another person, each with full authority to enter the box, the co-lessee of the box can remove all of its contents; but that may not be possible if the bank learned of the death and sealed the box. If the decedent was the sole lessee of the safe deposit box, a Probate procedure is necessary in order to get possession of the contents of the box.

If you believe that the value of the contents of the box is nominal, it will still take a Court order before you will be allowed to access the box. As explained in Chapter 3, you can get a Court order giving you permission to inspect the contents of the box and remove the Will, any insurance policy and the deed to the burial plot. If the box contains other items, ask the bank to make an inventory of the contents of the safe deposit box for you to give to the Court.

Whether the contents of the box can be removed by Affidavit or by a Voluntary Administrator with a Short Certificate depends on the value of the Estate. If the value of the contents of the box exceed the amount allowed under these procedures, you need to consult with an attorney to assist you with a full Probate procedure.

If there is a full Probate procedure, a Personal Representative will be appointed by the Probate Court. The Court will issue Letters giving the Personal Representative authority to take possession of the decedent's assets. The Personal Representative can present the Letters to the bank or safe deposit box lessor, and they will give the Personal Representative free access to the safe deposit box.

TRANSFERRING REAL PROPERTY

No Probate procedure is necessary to transfer real property if the decedent held that property:

➪   as the owner of a Life Estate - or -

➪   jointly with rights of survivorship - or -

➪   as Tenants by the Entirety

The survivor joint owner or the remainder beneficiary of the Life Estate owns the property as of the date of death, however, the decedent's name remains on the deed. Anyone examining title to the property will not know of the death. The New York Department of Health is responsible to issue the death certificate, but not to publish it or make it part of the public record.

You can have a death certificate recorded in the county where the property is located, however if you later sell the property the buyer will want to be assured that there are no taxes that might be a lien on the property as a result of the decedent's death. The closing could be delayed while the closing agent scrambles to obtain a tax release from the New York Department of Taxation. If you are the surviving joint owner you can avoid this problem by having your accountant or attorney apply for a release from the Department of Taxation. When it is received you can have the release recorded along with the death certificate.

Even if you don't intend to sell the property, it is important that you take care of these matters soon after the decedent's death. If you don't, whoever inherits the property from you will need to get two tax releases, one for you and one for the decedent. That could be difficult to do if many years have passed since the decedent's death, and his tax records have been lost or destroyed.

Each state regulates the transfer of real property within that state. Many states do not require any document be recorded to transfer real property to a joint tenant who has a right of survivorship, or to a remainder beneficiary of a Life Estate interest. All the surviving owner need do is keep a certified copy of the death certificate available to produce at closing when the property is transferred.

Some states, including New York, allow the death certificate to be recorded in the county where the property is located, so that anyone examining title to the property will know who now owns the property. In other states, an Affidavit of Survivorship is recorded along with the death certificate. If the decedent owned out of state real property jointly with rights of survivorship, or if he held a Life Estate interest, you may want to call the recording department in the county where the property is located to find out what documents (if any) need to be recorded to let people know that the surviving joint tenant (or remainder beneficiary) now owns the property. In New York, the Office of the Clerk or the Register is in charge of recording deeds. In other states, it might be the Clerk of the Circuit Court, or the County Recorder.

Of course, if the decedent owned real property in his own name or as a Tenant In Common, you need to contact an attorney in that state to have the property transferred to the proper beneficiary.

There needs to be a full Probate proceeding if the decedent left real property in his name only or as a Tenant In Common; or if he left personal property worth more than $20,000. The proceeding can take anywhere from several months to more than a year depending on the size and complexity of the Probate Estate. A Personal Representative must be appointed and Letters issued.

APPOINTING THE PERSONAL REPRESENTATIVE

New York statute gives an order of priority in the appointment of a Personal Representative. Whoever the decedent named as Personal Representative or Executor of his Will has top priority. If that person is unable or unwilling to serve, the person named in the Will as an alternate or successor Personal Representative has priority.

If none of these are willing or able to serve, the residuary beneficiaries of the Estate have the right to be appointed as Personal Representative. If there is disagreement over who should serve, the Court will decide who is best suited to settle the Estate (Surr. Ct. Proc. 1418).

New York statute (Surr. Ct. Proc. 1001) gives an order of priority of appointment for those who die without a Will:
1st spouse   2nd children   3rd grandchildren
4th father or mother   5th brother or sister
6th anyone who is entitled to the largest share
     of the Estate and who is qualified to serve.

Whoever wishes to serve as Personal Representative must be at least 18 years of age and must be approved by the Probate Court. In general, the Court will not appoint someone who lives in another state, unless a resident of New York agrees to serve as Co-Personal Representative (Surr. Ct. Proc. Act 707).

YOUR RIGHTS AS A BENEFICIARY

The Personal Representative is in charge of settling the Estate. Too often, beneficiaries of the Estate have no idea of what is going on. They wait to receive their inheritance, not knowing that they have rights under New York law; and more importantly, not knowing how to assert their rights.

✧ RIGHT TO BE KEPT INFORMED

Anyone who has an interest in the Estate has the right to be kept informed, beginning with the name and address of the Personal Representative and his attorney (Surr. Ct. Proc. Act 1409). You have the right to receive a copy of the Will and to raise an objection if you have any concern for the validity of the Will (Surr. Ct. Proc. Act 1410).

As the Probate progresses, you have the right to receive an accounting of how money is spent and how the Personal Representative intends to distribute the property once all the bills, expenses and taxes are paid. Write a letter to the attorney for the Personal Representative requesting copies of all documents filed with the Court.

✧ RIGHT TO YOUR OWN ATTORNEY

The attorney who handles the Estate is employed by, and represents, the Personal Representative. If the Estate is sizeable, you might consider employing your own attorney to check that things are done properly and in a timely manner. Even if the Estate is small, consider consulting with an attorney any time you are concerned about the way the Probate is being conducted.

✧ RIGHT TO OBJECT TO PERSONAL REPRESENTATIVE

Regardless of who has priority to serve, it is the Court who has final say as to who will serve as Personal Representative. You have the right to object to the appointment of a Personal Representative for any of the following reasons:

⇨ he is under the age of 18, or
⇨ he is a convicted felon, or
⇨ his is not fit to serve because of substance abuse or dishonesty, or
⇨ he does not have the ability to understand the Probate procedure, or
⇨ he is unable to read or write the English language (Surr. Ct. Proc. Act 707, 709).

If the Judge agrees with your objection, he can appoint someone who is acceptable to those who have a majority interest in the Estate. If you lose the battle over who is going to be appointed as Personal Representative, you still have the right to ask the Court to supervise the activities of the Personal Representative by giving him Letters that limit or restrict the things that he can do without Court approval. For example, you could ask that the Personal Representative not be allowed to sell certain of the decedent's assets without Court approval (Surr. Ct. Proc. Act 702).

✧ RIGHT TO APPEAR BEFORE THE COURT

You have the right to go before the Court on your own, and raise an objection to any aspect of the Probate proceeding, however before doing so, you should consult with an experienced Probate attorney. He can explain the best way for you to present your concerns to the Court. He can tell you what arguments have a good chance of swaying the Judge. And he can tell you which arguments have so little probability of success that they are not worth pursuing.

❖ RIGHT TO DEMAND BOND

It doesn't happen often, but every now and again a Personal Representative will run off with Estate funds. A bond is insurance for the Estate. If Estate monies are stolen, the company that issued the bond will reimburse the Estate for the loss. In general, the Court will not require a bond unless the decedent's Will says the Personal Representative needs to obtain a bond (Surr. Ct. Proc. Act 806).

Most Wills state that no bond shall be required. The reason is two-fold. The Will maker chooses someone he trusts to administer the Estate, so he does not think a bond is necessary. And there are economic reasons. The cost of the bond is paid for by the Estate, and ultimately the amount inherited is reduced by the amount paid for the bond.

If there is no Will, the Court will require bond in an amount equal to the value of all personal property (stocks, bonds, bank accounts, etc.) (Surr. Ct. Proc. Act 801). To save money, beneficiaries of the Estate may decide to file a request with the Court to waive bond. However, the cost of the bond should not be a factor if there is any danger of the Estate property belong lost or mismanaged.

If you are concerned about the safety of the Estate assets, it is important that you not sign a waiver, but rather ask the Court to order the Personal Representative be bonded.

✦ RIGHT TO KNOW PERSONAL REPRESENTATIVE'S FEES

The Personal Representative is entitled to be compensated for his efforts in settling the Estate. If he is also a beneficiary of the Estate he may decide not to take a commission and just take his inheritance. The reason may be economic. Any fee the Representative takes is taxable as ordinary income, but monies inherited are not taxable to him as a beneficiary. Ask the Personal Representative to tell you, in writing, whether he intends to charge a fee, and if so, how much.

There are statutory guidelines for what is "reasonable" compensation. Under New York statute, compensation is based on the amount received as Probate property and then paid out from the Estate:

> 5% commission on receiving and
>   paying out the first $100,000;
> 4% commission on the next $200,000;
> 3% commission on the next $700,000;
> 2 1/2 % on the next 4 million;
> 2% on anything over 5 million dollars.

The Court can increase the amount due to the Personal Representative for any extraordinary service performed in settling the Estate and the Court can decrease the statutory value if the Court finds that the Representative acted unreasonably or caused unnecessary delays (Surr. Ct. Proc. Act 2307).

✧ RIGHT TO KNOW THE ATTORNEY'S FEES

It is the Personal Representative's job to use the Probate Estate to pay all valid claims and then to distribute what is left to the proper beneficiary. Debts are paid from the decedent's Estate and not from the pocket of the Personal Representative. However, if he fails to use reasonable care and diligence, he may be responsible to pay for any harm he causes (Est. Powers & Trusts 11-4.7).

The Personal Representative has the right to employ an attorney to guide him through the Probate procedure so that things will be done properly and at no personal cost to the Representative. It is proper to have the attorney paid with Estate funds.

You, as a beneficiary of the Estate, have the right to know how much will be charged for legal fees. Ask the Personal Representative to give you a copy of the retainer agreement. If the attorney is employed on an hourly basis, have the attorney give a written estimate of the time he expects to spend on the Probate proceeding.

There is no statutory guideline for what is a "reasonable" fee for the attorney, but in general, they much the same as that of those of the Personal Representative. As with the Personal Representatives fees, whatever fee is charged is subject to Court approval (Surr. Ct. Proc. Act 2110).

✧   RIGHT TO COPY OF INVENTORY

Within six months of his appointment, the Personal Representative must prepare an inventory of all of the assets in the decedent's *Gross Taxable Estate*. He will make a list of assets of the Probate Estate and another list of items that pass outside of Probate such as property owned jointly with rights of survivorship, or property contained in the decedent's Revocable Living Trust (Uniform Rules for Surrogate's Court No. 207.20).

The value of the inventory is used to determine how much taxes need to be paid. The value of the Probate Estate is used to determine the Personal Representative's fee. It is important that you receive a copy of the inventory, and that you are satisfied with the value assigned to each item.

✧   RIGHT TO AN APPRAISAL

The Personal Representative can employ an appraiser to assist in determining the value of items included in the Estate inventory — but he is not required to have an appraisal unless ordered by the Court. If you are not satisfied with the value assigned to any Probate asset, you have the right to ask the Personal Representative to have the item appraised. If he refuses, you can ask the Court to order an independent appraisal of the item.

✧ RIGHT TO AN ACCOUNTING

Before closing the Estate the Personal Representative must file an accounting of how Estate funds were spent, and how the Representative intends to distribute whatever is left (Surr. Ct. Proc. Act 2203, 2005). If the Estate has significant assets you may want your own accountant to look over the accounting. If there are any problems that your accountant can not resolve with the Personal Representative, you can raise these issues with the Court.

✧ RIGHT TO HAVE THE ESTATE CLOSED WITHOUT DELAY

How long it takes to complete the Probate proceeding depends on the size and complexity of the matter. Unless there is some unusual circumstance, such as a Court battle over some part of the Probate proceeding, the Estate should be closed within one year from the date of death. If an Estate Tax return has been filed, the Estate should be closed within 90 days after the receipt of the state and federal tax release.

If you do not receive an accounting and a proposed plan of distribution within these time periods, you have the right to ask the Court to order the Personal Representative to file an accounting and proceed with the settlement of the Estate (Surr. Ct. Proc. Act 2205, 2206)

✧ RIGHT TO RECEIVE A DEBT FREE INHERITANCE

Once a beneficiary finally receives his inheritance, about the last thing he wants to hear is that there is some unfinished business, or worse yet that monies need to be paid from the inheritance he received. But that is just what could happen if the Personal Representative distributes the money before all the creditors are paid.

The Personal Representative is not required to publish notice to creditors that they have the right to come forward and present any claim they have against the Estate. If he does not publish such notice, after seven months he can distribute the monies to the beneficiaries and the creditor cannot sue the Personal Representative (Surr. Ct. Proc. Act 1802).

Taxes are another concern. You should ask to see a copy of all of the tax returns that were filed, and then verify that any monies that were due have been paid. Most importantly, you should not agree to having the Estate closed if the closing statement shows that there are any outstanding debts that need to be paid.

IT'S YOUR RIGHT - DON'T BE INTIMIDATED

You may feel uncomfortable being assertive with a friend or family member who is Personal Representative. Don't be. It's your money and your right to be informed. Be especially firm if the Personal Representative waves you off with "You've known me for years. Surely you trust me." People who are trustworthy, don't ask to be trusted. They do what is right. The very fact that the Personal Representative is resisting, is a red flag. In such situation, you can explain that it is not a matter of trust, but a matter of what is your legal right.

At the same time, keep things in perspective. Your relationship with the Personal Representative may be more important to you than the money you inherit. The job of settling an Estate can be complex and demanding. If the Personal Representative is getting the job done, let him know you appreciate his efforts.

THE CHECK LIST

We discussed many things that need to be done when someone dies in the state of New York. The next page contains a check list that you may find helpful.

You can check those items that you need to do, and then cross them off the list once they are done. We made the list as comprehensive as possible, so many items may not apply in your case. In such case, you can cross them off the list or mark them *N/A* (not applicable).

Things To Do

FUNERAL ARRANGEMENTS TO BE MADE
☐ AUTOPSY ☐ ANATOMICAL GIFT
☐ DISPOSITION OF BODY OR ASHES

DEATH CERTIFICATE
☐ HAVE CERTIFICATE RECORDED
GIVE COPY TO: _____
_____

NOTICE OF DEATH
PEOPLE TO BE NOTIFIED _____

COMPANIES TO NOTIFY
☐ TELEPHONE COMPANY
    ☐ LOCAL CARRIER   ☐ LONG DISTANCE   ☐ CELLULAR
☐ NEWSPAPER (OBITUARY PRINTED)
☐ NEWSPAPER DELIVERY CANCELLED   ☐ deposit refund
☐ SOCIAL SECURITY
☐ INTERNET SERVER CANCELLED
☐ TELEVISION CABLE/SATELLITE COMPANY CANCELLED
☐ POWER & LIGHT   ☐ deposit refund
☐ POST OFFICE
☐ OTHER UTILITIES (GAS, WATER)   ☐ deposit refund
☐ PENSION PLAN
☐ ANNUITY
☐ HEALTH INSURANCE COMPANY
☐ LIFE INSURANCE COMPANY
☐ HOME INSURANCE COMPANY
☐ MOTOR VEHICLE INSURANCE COMPANY
☐ CONDOMINIUM OR HOMEOWNER ASSOCIATION
☐ CANCEL SERVICE CONTRACT   ☐ deposit refund
☐ CREDIT CARD COMPANIES
    _____
    _____
    _____

Things To Do

REMOVE DECEDENT AS BENEFICIARY OF:

☐ WILL   ☐ INSURANCE POLICY   ☐ PENSION PLAN
☐ BANK OR IRA ACCOUNT   ☐ SECURITY

DEBTS

PAY DECEDENT'S DEBTS (AMOUNT & CREDITOR)

_____

COLLECT MONIES OWED TO DECEDENT (AMOUNT & DEBTOR)

_____

TAXES

☐ FILE FINAL FEDERAL INCOME TAX RETURN
☐ FILE FINAL STATE INCOME TAX RETURN
☐ RECEIVE INCOME TAX REFUND
☐ FILE ESTATE TAX RETURN

PROPERTY TO BE TRANSFERRED

☐ PERSONAL EFFECTS
☐ MOTOR VEHICLE
☐ BANK ACCOUNT
☐ CREDIT UNION ACCOUNT
☐ IRA ACCOUNT
☐ SECURITIES
☐ BROKERAGE ACCOUNT
☐ INSURANCE PROCEEDS
☐ HOMESTEAD
☐ TIME SHARE
☐ OTHER REAL PROPERTY
☐ CONTENTS OF SAFE DEPOSIT BOX

OTHER THINGS TO DO

_____
_____
_____

WHAT TO KEEP — WHAT TO THROW AWAY

Once the Probate proceeding is over, you will be left with many documents and wonder which you need to keep:

COURT DOCUMENTS

You should keep a copy of the inventory to establish the value of property that you inherit. That value becomes your basis for any Capital Gains Tax that you may need to pay in the future. Other than the inventory, there is no reason to keep any Court document, provided you are satisfied with the way things were done; and do not intend to take action against the Personal Representative, or his attorney. The Clerk of the Probate Court keeps the Probate file on record, so if for some reason you later need a copy of a Probate document, you can get it from the Clerk.

PERSONAL RECORDS

The surviving spouse, or if no spouse, his next of kin should keep the decedent's personal papers (birth certificate, marriage certificate, naturalization papers, army records, religious documents, etc.). They may be needed in order to apply for government, or other, benefits. The next of kin may want to keep the decedent's medical records in the event that a family member needs to check out a genetic disorder.

TAX RECORDS

The IRS has up to three years to collect additional taxes, and you have up to seven years to claim a loss from a worthless security, so you should keep the decedent's tax file for seven years from the date of filing the return. You can learn more about which records to keep from the IRS publication 552. You can get the publication by calling the IRS at (800) 829-3676 or you can download it from their Web site: http://www.irs.gov

Everyman's Estate Plan 7

The first six chapters of this book describe how to wind up the affairs of the decedent. As you read those chapters, you learned about the kinds of problems that can occur when settling the decedent's Estate. It is relatively simple for you to set up an Estate Plan so that your family members are not burdened with similar problems. An *Estate Plan* is the arranging of your finances for maximum control and protection during your lifetime, and at the same time ensuring that your property will be transferred quickly and at little cost to your heirs.

If you think that only wealthy people need to prepare an Estate Plan, you are mistaken. Each year, heirs of relatively modest Estates, spend thousands of dollars to settle an Estate. A bit of planning could have eliminated most, if not all, of the expense and hassle suffered by those families.

The suggestions in this chapter are designed to assist the average person in preparing a practical and inexpensive Estate Plan, so we named this chapter EVERYMAN'S ESTATE PLAN.

Once you create your own Estate Plan, you can be assured that your family will not be left with more problems than happy memories of you.

AVOIDING PROBATE

After reading the last Chapter, many will come to the conclusion that Probate is a good thing to avoid. Those who have $20,000 and no real property may not be concerned with avoiding Probate because as explained, your beneficiaries can get possession of that property with little effort or expense.

But if you own real property, in your name only, in excess of $20,000, a full Probate will be necessary with all of its inherent delays and expenses. Notice that the operative phrase in the last sentence is *in your name only*. Whether Probate is necessary depends on how your property is titled (owned). It makes no difference whether you do or do not have a Will. If you own property in excess of $20,000 ($30,000 if you are married) and that property is in your name only, your beneficiaries will need to go through a Probate procedure in order to get possession of that property.

As explained in Chapter 5, there are many ways to title real property so that it passes automatically without the need for Probate. For example, if you own real property jointly with rights of survivorship, upon your death, the survivors will own the property without the need to go through Probate. Similarly if you own a Life Estate, upon your death, the property passes directly to the remainder beneficiary.

In this Chapter we will examine ways to title your personal property (bank accounts, securities, cars, etc.) so that it passes to your beneficiaries without the need for Probate.

You can arrange to have all of your bank accounts set up so that should you die, the money goes directly to a beneficiary. For example, suppose all you own is a bank account and you want whatever you have in the account to go to your son and daughter when you die. You might think that a simple solution is to put each child's name on the account as joint tenants with right of survivorship, but first consider the problems associated with a joint account.

⊠ POTENTIAL LIABILITY
If you hold a bank account jointly with your adult child and that child is sued or gets a divorce, the child may need to disclose his ownership of the joint account. In such a case, you may find yourself spending money to prove that the account was established for your convenience only and that all of the money in that account really belongs to you.

⊠ OVERREACHING
If you set up a joint account with your child so that the child has authority to withdraw funds from the account, monies could be withdrawn without your knowledge or consent.

If you open a multiple party account with two of your children, there is the problem of what happens to the funds after your death. Should you die, your share of the account belongs to the surviving joint owners, equally. But as a practical matter each joint owner has free access to the joint account. After your death the first child to the bank may decide to withdraw all of the money and that will, at the very least, cause hard feelings between them.

THE IN TRUST FOR ACCOUNT

If you open an account *In Trust For* ("ITF") someone, unless your contract with the bank states differently:

⇨ During your lifetime you are free to add to the account account, or even close it, without asking the beneficiary's permission to do so.

⇨ The beneficiary has no right to make withdrawals from the account during your lifetime.

⇨ If you hold the account In Trust For two or more beneficiaries, the funds will be divided equally among the beneficiaries who survive you. (Est. Powers & Trusts 7-5.1, 7-5.2, 7-5.7).

You can set up an account that you hold jointly with your spouse so that it is held "In Trust For" one or more beneficiaries. For example:

Eldon Smith and Lorraine Smith,
as JOINT TENANTS WITH RIGHT OF SURVIVORSHIP
IN TRUST FOR Eldon Smith, Jr. and Fred Smith

Unless your contract with the bank states differently, under New York law:

⇨ The children (Eldon, Jr. and Fred) have no right to the account during the lifetime of their parents.

⇨ If either Eldon or Lorraine dies, the surviving spouse owns the account, and is free to close the account or change the beneficiary of the account.

⇨ Once Eldon and Lorraine are deceased, their sons share the money in the account equally.

⇨ If one of the children dies before the surviving parent dies, the remaining son gets all of the money in the account (Banking 675, Est. Powers & Trusts 7-5.6).

THE TRANSFER ON DEATH SECURITY

Many states have laws allowing companies to offer securities with a **Pay On Death** ("POD") or **Transfer On Death** ("TOD") to a named beneficiary. The laws relating to a POD or TOD designation are much like the laws relating to New York's ITF account, namely, the named beneficiary has no right to the security during the lifetime of the owner. Once the owner of the security dies, the security is transferred to the beneficiary without the need for Probate.

As of this printing in 2005, New York has no laws relating to POD or TOD securities, however, if you are purchasing a security and the company offers such designation, you may want to investigate all of the terms and conditions of such a designation, including their policy as it relates to the transfer of securities to a minor.

If your Estate consists only of bank accounts, and you want all of your property to go to one or two beneficiaries without the need for Probate, but with maximum control and protection of your funds during your lifetime, then holding your property "In Trust For" the beneficiary should accomplish your goal.

GIFT TO A MINOR CHILD

At the beginning of this chapter, we identified two problems with a joint account: potential liability if the joint owner is sued and overreaching by the joint owner. If you wish to make a gift to a minor child, that presents still another problem. The "In Trust For" account avoids the problem of potential liability and overreaching, but if the beneficiary of such account is a minor, there is the problem of the child having access to a large sum of money.

If the amount in the account is $10,000 or less, the monies can be paid to the child's parent or Guardian, for the use and benefit of the child. If the amount exceeds $10,000, the company will not transfer the funds without authorization from the Court (Est. Powers & Trusts 7-5.3). The Court may decide that it is necessary to appoint a Guardian to care for the child's property.

You may think it best that the child inherits more than $10,000 — this way a Court will see to it that the monies are held safely till the child is an adult. But that only presents a new set of problems. It takes time, effort and money to set up a Guardianship. If you leave the child a significant amount of money, the Guardian has the right to be paid to manage those funds. It could happen that the cost of the Guardianship significantly reduces the amount of money inherited by the child.

There are ways to avoid the problem of having a Guardian appointed to care for property inherited by a child, and yet ensuring that the monies are protected. One such method is the New York UNIFORM TRANSFERS TO MINORS ACT.

THE UNIFORM TRANSFERS TO MINORS ACT

The **New York Uniform Transfers to Minors Act** is designed to protect gifts made to a minor by appointing someone to be the **Custodian** of a gift until the child is an adult. For example, you can make a minor child the beneficiary of your life insurance policy and name a trusted relative or friend to be the Custodian of the gift. Should you die while the child is a minor, the insurance company will give the proceeds of the policy to the person you named as Custodian to hold until the child is an adult.

You can make a gift to a minor in your Will. You can appoint your Personal Representative (or anyone else) as Custodian of the gift. For example:

I give the sum of $20,000 to_____ (name) as custodian for _____ (name of minor) under the New York Uniform Transfers to Minors Act.

In general, the Custodian must distribute the gift when the child reaches 18; however, gifts made by Will can be held by the Custodian until the child is 21.

THE LIFETIME GIFT

You can even use the New York Uniform Transfers to Minors Law to make a gift during your lifetime of some item such as shares in a corporation. You can nominate yourself as Custodian of the gift, or you can name another person to serve as Custodian. Once the lifetime gift is made it becomes irrevocable, so this method is not appropriate unless you are sure that you want the child to have the gift once he/she reaches the age of 18 (Estates 7-6.3, 7-6.9, 7-6.11, 7-6.21).

The Custodian needs to invest and manage the property in a responsible, prudent manner. He must keep records of all transactions made with custodial property; and make those records available for inspection. If he doesn't give a regular accounting , the child's parent, or Guardian, or even the child, if he is at least 14 can ask the Court to order an accounting (Est. Powers & Trusts 7-6.14, 7-6.19).

The Custodian has the discretion to use the gift to care for the child. The Custodian can pay monies directly to the child, or can use the money for the child's benefit. The Custodian can refuse to use any of the monies for the child and just keep the funds invested until the time of distribution. If the Custodian wants to keep the funds invested the child's parent, or Guardian, or the child once he is 14, can ask the Judge to order the Custodian to part with some or all of the money for the benefit of the child. The Judge will decide what is in the child's best interest and then rule on the matter.

The Custodian is entitled to be paid for his effort each year. If the gift is sizeable, the Custodian's fee can be sizeable. Before appointing a person or a financial institution as Custodian, it is best to come to a written agreement about what will be charged to manage custodial property (Est. Powers & Trusts 7-6.15)

A gift made under the New York Uniform Transfers to Minors Act is limited to one minor only (Estates 7-6.10, 7-6.15). If you want to give a single gift, such as a gift of real property to two or more children or if you want more flexibility about when the minor is to receive the gift, then a Trust may be the better way to go.

We will discuss Trusts later in this chapter.

THE GIFT OF REAL PROPERTY

As explained in Chapter 5, if you own real property together with another, then who owns the property upon your death depends on how the Grantee is identified on the face of the deed. If you compare the Grantee clause of the deed to the examples given in Chapter 5, you can determine who will inherit the property should you die. If you are not satisfied with the way the property will be inherited, you need to consult with an attorney to change the deed so that it will conform to your wishes.

If you own the property in your name only, when you die, there will need to be a Probate proceeding to determine the proper beneficiary of that parcel of land. If your main objective is to avoid Probate, you can have an attorney change the deed so that upon your death, the property will descend to your beneficiary without the need for Probate. As with bank and securities accounts there are different ways to do so, each with its own advantages and disadvantages.

JOINT OWNERSHIP

If you hold property in your name only, and wish to avoid Probate, you can have your deed changed so that you and a beneficiary are joint owners with rights of survivorship. If you do so, should either of you die, the other will own the property 100%. That avoids Probate, but by making that person joint owner, you are, in effect, making a gift of half of the property during your lifetime. You will not be able to sell that property without the beneficiary's permission. And if the beneficiary gives permission and the property is sold, the beneficiary will have the legal right to half of the proceeds of the sale. As explained on the next page, you may be creating tax problems as well.

You can arrange to sell your home without paying a Capital Gains Tax (see page 40), but if you make someone joint owner of your home who does not live with you, a Capital Gains Tax may need to be paid on the joint owner's share of the proceeds should you decide to sell the property.

CAUTION — GIFT OF HOMESTEAD

Some elderly parents worry that they may need nursing care at some time in the future and lose all of their life savings to pay for that care. The parent may decide that the best way to avoid Probate and protect the homestead from loss is to transfer the homestead to their child with the understanding that the parent will continue to live there until he/she dies. But this is just trading risks.

⊠ RISK OF LOSS

Property transferred to your child could be lost if the child runs into serious financial difficulties or gets sued. This is especially a risk if your child is a professional doctor, nurse, accountant, financial planner, attorney, etc.). If your child is (or gets) married, this complicates matters even more so. If the child is divorced, the property may need to be included as part of the settlement agreement. This may be to your child's detriment because the child may need to share the value of the property with his/her former spouse. If you do not transfer the property, it cannot become part of the marital equation.

⊠ LOSS OF HOMESTEAD TAX EXEMPTION

People who own and occupy a residence in New York are entitled to a **School Tax Relief Exemption ("STAR")**. The exempt amount is determined annually (Real Prop. Tax 425). In addition to STAR, persons of low income who are 65 or older and/or have a disability are entitled to have a certain percentage of their assessed valuation exempt from property taxes (Real Prop. Tax 467, 459, 459-c). If you transfer your homestead, you will lose your right to receive these tax breaks.

⊠ LOSS OF HOMESTEAD CREDITOR PROTECTION

Up to $10,000 of the value of your homestead is protected from creditors during your lifetime. This may not seem like much, but it could keep a roof over your head if the equity in your home is under $10,000. For example, suppose your home is worth $100,000 and you have a mortgage of $90,000. With the exception of property taxes and the loan on your homestead, none of your creditors can force the sale of your property (C.P.L.R. 5206).

If you simply transfer your homestead to a child, you lose your homestead protection against creditors. If you are married, it is a double loss of creditor protection. Not only do you lose creditor protection for yourself, you lose it for your spouse as well (see Page 97).

If the child does not occupy that property as his homestead, there is no homestead creditor protection whatsoever. The child's creditors can force the sale of the property (that's your home) for relatively small amounts of unpaid debts.

☒   POSSIBLE GIFT TAX

If the value of the transfer is worth more than $11,000 you need to file a Gift Tax return. For most of us, this is not a problem because no Gift Tax need be paid unless the value of the property (plus the value of all gifts in excess of the Annual Gift Tax Exclusion that you gave over your lifetime) exceeds $1,000,000 (see Chapter 3). But if your Estate is in that tax bracket, you need to be aware that you are "using up" your lifetime Gift Tax Exclusion.

☒   POSSIBLE CAPITAL GAINS TAX

Although Congress has expressed their intent to phase out the Estate Tax, there is no discussion to do away with the Capital Gains Tax. If you gift the property to the child during your lifetime, when he sells the property he will pay a Capital Gains Tax on the increase in value from the price you paid for your home to the selling price at the time your child sells the property.

If you do not make the gift during your lifetime, the child will inherit the property with a step-up in basis, i.e., he will inherit the property at its market value as of your date of death. Under today's tax structure and continuing until 2009, that step-up in basis is unlimited. If your child sells the property when he inherits it, he will pay no Capital Gains Tax, regardless of how large the step-up in basis.

In 2010, there will be a limit on the amount that can be inherited free of the Capital Gains Tax; but that limit is quite high, so for most of us this is not a concern.

⊠ POSSIBLE LOSS OF GOVERNMENT BENEFITS

If you transfer property, then depending upon the value of the transfer, you could be disqualified from receiving Medicaid or Supplemental Security Income ("SSI") benefits for a substantial period of time. When a person applies for Medicaid, he must disclose if, within three years of his application, he transferred property for less than the full value (i.e. he gifted property).

This reporting period extends to five years if the transfer was to a Trust. The Medicaid agency will compute a disqualification period depending on the value of the transfer. This can present a serious problem should you need extended nursing care during that period of time.

Under current state and federal law, there are many ways to protect your homestead and still qualify for government benefits. Before transferring your homestead because of your concern for the cost of future health care, consult with an Elder Law attorney. He will be able to suggest ways to protect your assets, and still ensure that you receive the health care that you may require in your later years.

THE LIFE ESTATE, NOT A COMPLETE SOLUTION

Some of the problems we have discussed regarding an outright gift of the homestead, can be avoided by transferring the home but keeping a Life Estate for yourself. However, even though you keep a Life Estate, there still are tax issues and concerns regarding shared control of the property. Before making any transfer of real property, it is important to consult with an Elder Law attorney and/or certified financial planner and/or accountant, to examine all aspects related to the transfer.

 **LAWYER**   OUT OF STATE PROPERTY

Each state is in charge of the way property located in that state is transferred. If you own property in another state (or country) then you need to consult with an attorney in that state (or country) to determine how that property will be transferred to your beneficiaries once you die. Many state laws are similar to New York, namely, property held as JOINT TENANTS WITH RIGHT OF SURVIVOR or a LIFE ESTATE INTEREST are transferred without the need for Probate.

If you own property in another state in your name only, or as a TENANT IN COMMON, or if you hold property with your spouse in a Community Property state, a Probate procedure may need to be held in that state. If it is necessary to have a Probate procedure in New York, then a second Probate procedure may need to be held in the state where the property is located. This could significantly increase the cost of Probate.

Still another problem is the matter of taxes. Inheritance taxes may be due in the state where the property is held. It may be necessary to file a tax return in two states. In addition to increased taxes, this can double the cost of the accounting fees.

You may wish to consult with an attorney for suggestions about how to set up your Estate Plan to avoid such problems.

A full Probate procedure may be necessary if you hold property in your name only or as a Tenant In Common. We explored different ways to re-title property to avoid Probate, but these methods may have trade-offs that are unacceptable to you. One way to avoid many of these potential problems is to set up a ***Revocable Living Trust*** (also known as an *Inter Vivos Trust*).

A Revocable Living Trust is designed to care for your property during your lifetime and then to distribute your property once you die without the need for Probate. You may have been encouraged to set up such a Trust by your financial planner, or attorney, or accountant. Even people of modest means are being encouraged to use a Trust as the basis of their Estate Plan. But Trusts have their pros and cons. Before getting into that, let's first discuss what a Trust is and how it works:

SETTING UP A TRUST

To create a Trust, an attorney prepares the Trust document in accordance with the client's needs and desires. The person who signs the document is called the *Trustor* or *Settlor.* If the *Trustor* also funds the Trust, then he is also referred to as the ***Grantor.*** We will refer to the Revocable Living Trust as the "Living Trust" or just the "Trust" and the person setting up the Trust as the "Grantor." The Trust document identifies who is to be the Trustee (manager) of property placed in the Trust. Usually the Grantor appoints himself as Trustee so that he is in total control of property that he places into the Trust. The Trust document also names a Successor Trustee who will take over the management of the Trust property should the Trustee resign, or become disabled or die.

Once the Trust document is properly signed, the Grantor transfers property into the Trust. The Grantor does this by changing the name on the account from his individual name to his name as Trustee. For example, if Elaine Richards sets up a Trust naming herself as Trustee, and she wishes to place her bank account into the Trust then all she need do is instruct the bank to change the name on the account from Elaine Richards to:

ELAINE RICHARDS, TRUSTEE OF THE ELAINE RICHARDS REVOCABLE TRUST AGREEMENT DATED JULY 12, 2004.

When the change is made, all the money in the account becomes Trust property. Elaine (wearing her Trustee hat) has total control of the account, taking money out, and putting money in, as she sees fit. Similarly, if she wants to put real property into the Trust all she need do is have her attorney prepare a new deed with the owner identified as ELAINE RICHARDS, TRUSTEE (see page 117 for an example of real property placed into a Trust).

The Trust document states how the Trust property is to be managed during Elaine's lifetime. Should Elaine become disabled the Trust will provide for her Successor Trustee to take over and manage the Trust funds. Because the Trust is revocable, if she wishes, Elaine can terminate the Trust at any time and have all the Trust property returned and placed back into her own individual name. If she does not revoke her Trust during her lifetime, then once she dies the Trust becomes irrevocable, and her Successor Trustee must follow the terms of the Trust Agreement as written. If the Trust says to give the Trust property to certain beneficiaries, the Successor Trustee will do so, and without the need for Probate. If the Trust directs the Successor Trustee to continue to hold property in Trust and use the money to take care of a member of Elaine's family, then the Successor Trustee will do so.

Setting up a Trust has many good features.

☆☆ AVOID PROBATE

In New York, Probate can be time consuming and very expensive. Both the Personal Representative and his attorney are entitled to payment for their services. These fees can be significant. It may be necessary to employ accountants and appraisers, and real estate brokers to sell property as well. If you have property in two states, then two Probate procedures may be necessary (one in each state) and that could have the effect of doubling the cost of Probate. If the Trust is properly drafted and your property placed into the Trust, you should be able to avoid Probate altogether.

☆ FEDERAL ESTATE TAX SAVINGS

Many people think that the federal Estate Tax will be phased out so that by 2010, no Estate Taxes will be due regardless of the size of an Estate. But under current law in 2011, the Estate Tax is scheduled to be reinstated and those who own property worth more than $1,000,000 will once again be subject to a sizeable Estate Tax. And there still is the New York Estate Tax for an Estates in excess of $1,000,000.

A couple with a Taxable Estate in excess of a million dollars can reduce the risk of an Estate Tax by setting up a Trust, so that each partner can take advantage of his own Estate Tax Exclusion. For example, if a couple owns two million dollars, they can set up a Trust that separates the money into two Trusts once one partner dies. The Trust can be arranged so that the surviving spouse is free to use the income from both Trusts. Once both partners are deceased, the beneficiaries of their respective Trusts will inherit the funds, hopefully with no Estate Tax due. If the couple does not set up a Trust and continues to hold all of their property jointly, the last to die will own the two million dollars with only one Estate Tax Exclusion available.

☆ CARE FOR FAMILY MEMBER:

You can make provision in your Trust to care for a minor child or family member after you die. If your family member is immature or a born spender, and you are concerned that he may spend, within months, what took you a lifetime to earn, you can have your attorney prepare a Trust that will spread the inheritance over an extended period of time. Your Trust can direct the Trustee to give a certain amount of money every 5 or 10 years; for example you can direct the Trustee to give part of the gift when the beneficiary reaches 25, another amount when he reaches 35, and then 45, etc.

If your intended beneficiary has a creditor problem, you can set up a **Spendthrift Trust**. You can direct your Successor Trustee to use the Trust funds for your beneficiary's health care, education, and living expenses, and nothing else. With a properly drafted Spendthrift Trust provision the Trust funds should be protected from the claims of the creditors of the beneficiary.

NO CREDITOR PROTECTION FOR GRANTOR

You can set up a Spendthrift Trust for a beneficiary, but not for yourself. Because property held in your Revocable Living Trust is freely accessible to you, it is likewise accessible to your creditors both before and after your death. If you die owing money, your creditors can have a Personal Representative appointed to locate funds to pay those debts. The Personal Representative can require that your Trust property be used to pay for those debts (Est. Powers & Trusts 7-1.5, 7-3.1, Surr. Ct. Proc. Act 1002).

☆ PRIVACY

Your Trust is a private document. No one but your Successor Trustee and your beneficiaries need ever read it. If you make a gift of real property in your Will, your Personal Representative will have a certified copy of your Will recorded in the county in New York where the property is located (Surr. Ct. Proc. Act 2506). Once recorded, your Will becomes a public document. Anyone can examine the county records, read your Will and see who you did (or did not) provide for in your Will.

Even if your Will makes no gift of real property, once the Will is filed in the Probate Court it is open to public scrutiny — as are other Probate documents such as the inventory of your Probate Estate, creditor's claims, etc. In some states, court records are now available on the Internet!

LEASE SAFE DEPOSIT BOX AS TRUSTEE

Another privacy issue is what happens to the contents of your safe deposit box, should you become disabled or die. Under New York law, only the person who is leasing the safe deposit box can access that box. Once notified of your death, the bank will not allow anyone (even a joint tenant of the box) to remove the contents of the box without a Court order (Surr. Ct. Proc. Act 2003). Any member of your family can get a court order to examine the contents of your box under the supervision of a bank employee.

One of the benefits of having a Living Trust, is that you can lease the safe deposit box in your name as Trustee with instructions to the bank to allow your Successor Trustee free access to the safe deposit box in the event of your incapacity or death. By doing so you can avoid having the bank officer (or anyone other than your Successor Trustee) look at the contents of your safe deposit box.

☆☆ AVOID APPOINTMENT OF A GUARDIAN

Once you have a Trust you do not need to worry about who will take care of your property should you become disabled or too aged to handle your finances. The person you appoint as Successor Trustee will take over the care of the Trust property if you are unable to do so. If you do not make provision for the care of your property, it may be necessary for a Court to appoint a Guardian of your property. Guardianship is a good thing to avoid, not only because of the cost of the procedure, but also to avoid the embarrassment of a Court coming to the conclusion that you are not capable of managing your own finances.

Before appointing a Guardian, the Court will need to be convinced that you are unable to care for yourself. The judge will set a time for a competency hearing on the matter. Prior to the hearing, he will appoint a Court Evaluator to visit you and explain your rights under New York law. You can have your own attorney to represent you at the hearing. If you do not have an attorney, the Court may appoint one for you (Mental Hyg. 81.09, 81.10).

If the judge decides that you are incapacitated, he will appoint a Guardian of your person or property, or both. If a Guardian of your property is appointed he will take possession of your assets and file an inventory with the Court. The Court may order your Guardian to obtain a bond for the protection of your assets. Each year the Guardian must account to the Court for monies spent. Your Guardian may need to employ an accountant to help prepare the inventory and annual accounting (Mental Hyg. 81.25, 81.31, 81.32). Court filing fees, the cost of a bond, accounting fees, Guardian's fees, attorney's fees for you and the Guardian, are all paid from your Estate (that's your money!). And this expense goes on year after year until you are restored to capacity or die.

THE PROBLEMS

With all these perks, you may be ready to call your attorney to make an appointment to set up a Trust, but before doing so there are a few things you need to consider:

⊠ COST

Because of the thoroughness of the document and the fact that it is custom designed for you, a Trust will cost much more to draft than a simple Will. In addition to the initial cost of the Trust, it can be expensive to maintain the Trust should you become disabled or die. Your Successor Trustee has the right to charge for his duties as Trustee, as well as to charge for any specialized services performed. An attorney can charge to serve as Successor Trustee, and also charge for legal work he does on behalf of the Trust (Surr. Ct. Proc. Act 2309). to manage the Trust portfolio. Similarly a financial institution can charge for its services as Trustee, and also to manage the Trust portfolio.

You can choose an attorney, or an accountant, or a financial planner, to serve as Trustee, but this may create a conflict of interest because the professional can use his position as Trustee to generate fees. If you decide to appoint a professional as Trustee you should have a fee agreement stating what will be charged for his duties as Trustee and what will be charged for professional work done on behalf of the Trust. The fee agreement should be included in the Trust document with a provision that whoever accepts the job of Successor Trustee, agrees to accept the fee as provided in the Trust document.

You may decide to appoint your spouse or a family member as Successor Trustee, who may want little, or no, compensation. Regardless of who you choose to be Successor Trustee, you need come to a fee agreement. The agreement can be for a set amount or a percentage of the value of the Trust, or other method to be used to determine his compensation.

If you do not provide a fee schedule, then the Trustee is entitled to the amount as stated in Surr. Ct. Proc. Act 2309; and that fee is substantial. The Successor Trustee is entitled to 1% of the principal that he pays out, PLUS, each year he is entitled to an commission at the following rates:
$10.50 per $1,000 or major fraction thereof
on the first $400,000 of Principal of the Trust.

$4.50 per $1,000 or major fraction thereof
on the next $600,000 of Principal of the Trust.

$3.00 per $1,000 or major fraction thereof
on all additional Principal.

If you have Trust worth one million dollars your Successor Trustee is entitled to an annual commission of $6,900.
$10.50 X 400 = $4,200
$4.50 X 600 = $2,700
$4,200 + $2,700 = $6,900

If you instruct your Successor Trustee to immediately distribute the million dollars, he will still be entitled to $10,000 (1% of the Principal paid out).

⌧ COMPLEXITY

A Trust is a fairly complex document, often 20 pages long. It needs to be that long because you are establishing a vehicle for taking care of your property during your lifetime, as well as after your death. The Trust usually is written in "legalese," so it may take you considerable time and effort to understand it.

It is important to have your Trust document prepared by an attorney who has the patience to work with you until you fully understand each paragraph of the document and are satisfied that what it says is what you really want.

⌧ TAXES MAY STILL BE A PROBLEM

While you are operating the Trust as Trustee, all of the property held in your Revocable Living Trust is taxed as if you were holding that property in your own name. If the value of your Trust property exceeds the Estate and/or Gift Tax Exclusion value, taxes will be due and owing once you die.

For those in that fortunate tax bracket, an experienced financial planner or tax attorney can suggest other, more advanced, Estate Planning strategies to reduce taxes.

⊠   YOU MAY NEED YOUR SPOUSE'S PERMISSION
       TO TRANSFER PROPERTY INTO YOUR TRUST

Many married couples prepare a Trust as part of their overall Estate Plan. Sometimes a married person has a Trust that was prepared prior to the marriage, or he may decide to create a Trust to care for children from a previous marriage. In such case, it may be necessary to have the spouse agree, in writing, to transfers into the Trust. The reason permission is needed is the *Elective Share*. The Grantor's spouse has a right to inherit at least as much as allowed under New York law, unless the spouse signs a waiver, or a prenuptial or postnuptial agreement.

In New York, the Elective Share is equal to $50,000 or one-third of the *Net Estate* of the decedent spouse, whichever is greater. The Net Estate is the sum of:

⇨   Property held in the decedent's Trust, and
⇨   The Probate Estate less the cost of the Probate
       procedure; funeral expenses and all valid claims
       (but not including Estate Taxes); and
⇨   Non-probate transfers such as from joint bank
       accounts, "In Trust For" accounts,
       "Transfer On Death" securities, and
⇨   Gifts made by the decedent within one year of
       his death (Est. Powers & Trusts 5-1.1-A).

If the Net Estate is less than $50,000, the Elective Share is equal to the value of the Net Estate.

If you make transfers into your Trust without your spouse's permission, and without providing for the Elective Share, your surviving spouse can go to the Surrogates' Court and demand that as much property be transferred from the Trust (or from anyone in possession of your property) as is necessary to make up that Elective Share.

⊠ PROBATE MIGHT STILL BE NECESSARY

The Trust only works for those items that you place in the Trust. If you own property in your name only, then upon your death, a Probate procedure might be necessary in order to transfer the property to your beneficiary. For example, if you purchase a security in your name only, without a "Transfer On Death" designation to a named beneficiary or to your Trust, then a Probate procedure may be necessary to determine who should inherit the security.

The attorney who prepares the Trust usually creates a safety net for such situations. He prepares a Will for you to sign at the same time you sign the Trust. The Will makes your Trust the beneficiary of your Probate Estate. If you own anything in your name only and a Probate procedure is necessary, the Will directs your Personal Representative to make that asset part of your Trust by transferring the asset to your Successor Trustee. Your Successor Trustee will add that asset to your Trust (Est. Powers & Trusts 3-3.7).

The Will prepared by the attorney is called a "Pour Over Will" because it is designed to "pour" any asset titled in your name only, into the Trust. Having the Will ensures that all of your property will go to the beneficiaries named in your Trust. But the downside of holding property in your name only is that a full Probate procedure may be necessary just to get that asset into your Trust. If avoiding Probate is your goal, holding property, in your name only, defeats that goal.

You can ensure that a Probate procedure will not be necessary by transferring your assets into your Trust during your lifetime, but if you neglect to put something into your Trust, the Pour Over Will stands by to transfer that asset into your Trust.

⊠ ☆ THE TRUST IS LEGALLY ENFORCEABLE

Your Successor Trustee will take over the administration of your death upon your incapacity or death. Should there be a dispute regarding the administration of the Trust, your beneficiary, or your Successor Trustee, can ask the Court to settle the matter. For example, if the Trustee is abusing his power or not accounting for Trust funds, the beneficiaries can ask the Court to have the Trustee removed (Est. Powers & Trusts 7-2.6).

We gave this section a cross and a star, because the right to have a Trust enforced or administered by the Court is a double edged sword. It is great to have the Court protect the rights of your beneficiaries, but the cost of a court battle could be greater than if your Estate was subject to Probate in the first place. Your beneficiaries are at a financial disadvantage. The Court can require your Trustee to be personally liable for legal costs, but that only happens if the Trustee acted illegally or unreasonably. In most cases, the Trustee will be able to charge the expense of defending his actions to your Trust and your beneficiaries will pay for their legal expenses out of their own pockets. Win or lose, there will be just that much less for your beneficiaries to inherit.

Although all of the methods discussed in this Chapter can be used to transfer property without the need for Probate, it may be each method has a downside that is objectionable to you. Maybe you don't have enough money to warrant the cost of setting up the Trust at this time. Holding property jointly with another may raise issues of security and independence. Holding property so that it goes directly to a few beneficiaries in an In Trust For account, may not be as flexible as you wish.

This is especially the case if you wish to give gifts to several charities or to minor children instead of just one or two beneficiaries. For example, if you hold all your property so that it goes to your son without the need for Probate, and you ask him to use some of the money for your grandchild's education, it may be that your grandchild gets none of the money because your son is sued or falls upon hard times. If you keep your property in your name only and leave a Will giving a certain amount of money for your grandchild, the child will know exactly how much money you left and the purpose of that gift.

After taking into account all the pros and cons of avoiding Probate, you may well opt for a Will and a Probate procedure. If you make such a decision, it is important to keep in mind that Estate Planning is not an "all or nothing" choice. You can arrange your Estate so that certain items pass automatically to your intended beneficiary, and other items can be left in your name only, to be distributed as part of a Probate procedure. By arranging your finances in this manner, you can reduce the value of your Probate Estate, and that in turn should reduce the cost of Probate.

Your New York Will

Many people decide that the Will is the best route to go but do not act upon it, thinking it unnecessary to prepare a Will until they are very old and about to die. But according to reports published by the National Center for Health Statistics (a division of the U.S. Department of Health and Human Services) 2 of every 10 people who die in any given year are under the age of 60.

Twenty percent may seem like a small number until it hits close to home as it did with a young couple. They were having difficulty conceiving a child. They went from doctor to doctor until they met someone just beginning his practice. With his knowledge of the latest advances in medicine, he was able to help them.

The birth of their child was a moment of joy and gratitude. They asked a nurse to take a picture of them all together — the proud parents, the newborn child and the doctor who made it all possible. Happiness radiated from the picture, but within 6 months, one of them would be dead.

You might think it was the child. An infant's life is so fragile. SIDS and all manner of childhood diseases can threaten a little one. But no, he grew up a healthy young man.

If you looked at the picture, you might guess the husband. Overweight and stressed out; his ruddy complexion suggested high blood pressure. He looked like a typical heart- attack-prone type A personality.

No, he was fine and went on to enjoy raising his son.

Probably it was the wife. She had such a difficult time with the pregnancy and the delivery was especially hard. Maybe it was all too much for her.

No, she recovered and later had two more children.

It was the doctor who was killed in a collision with a truck.

WHY A WILL IS NECESSARY

Though we all agree, that one never knows, still people put off making a Will figuring that if they die before getting around to it, New York law will take over and their property will be distributed in the manner that they would have wanted anyway. The problem with that logic is the complexity of New York's Rules Governing Intestate Succession. It isn't difficult to figure out who will inherit your property, if you are survived by a spouse, child, parent or sibling. But if none of these survive you, the ultimate beneficiary of your property may not be the person you would have chosen, had you taken the time to do so.

Others think that it is not necessary to have a Will because they have arranged their finances so that all of their property will be inherited without the need for Probate. But money could come into your Estate after your death. This could happen in any number of ways from winning the lottery and dying (of happiness, no doubt) to receiving insurance funds after your death. For example, if you die in a house fire or flood the insurance company may need to pay for damage done to your property. In such case, a Personal Representative may need to be appointed and the monies distributed according to New York law.

If you die without a Will, the Personal Representative may not be the person you would have chosen. The monies may be distributed differently than you would have wished. And as explained in this Chapter, there are other important reasons to make a Will.

📑 MAKE GIFTS OF YOUR PERSONAL PROPERTY

Another benefit of making a Will is that you can make provision for who will get your personal property, including your car. If you make a gift of your car in your Will, it will be relatively simple for your car to be transferred to the beneficiary. If you do not make a *specific gift* of your car, it becomes part of your Probate Estate. Your Personal Representative will decide what to do with the car. He can sell it and include the proceeds of the sale in the Estate funds to be distributed to your residuary beneficiaries; or he can give the car to one beneficiary of your Estate as part of that beneficiary's share of the Estate.

SMALL GIFTS MATTER

Many who have lost someone close to them report that the distribution of small personal items caused the greatest conflict. If you arrange your finances so that no Probate procedure is necessary, your next of kin will need to decide how to distribute your personal effects. Without guidance from you and no Personal Representative with authority to make decisions, there could be disagreement and hard feelings, over items of little monetary value. If you make a Will, you can include a list of gifts of personal effects in your Will and your Personal Representative will distribute the gifts according to your directions.

Of course, you cannot list each and every item you own, but you can instruct your Personal Representative to allow certain family members to take their choice of items not mentioned in your Will. If two or more family members want the same item, have your Personal Representative use an appropriate lottery system (coin toss, high card in a cut of a deck of cards, etc.) to decide who "wins."

▤ MAKE ADJUSTMENT FOR PRIOR GIFTS

You can use your Will to make adjustments for gifts or loans given during your lifetime. For example, if you loaned money to a family member and do not expect to be repaid, you can deduct the loan from that person's inheritance. There is no need to make the adjustment if the borrower gives you a promissory note because should you die, the monies will be owed to your Estate and the Personal Representative can deduct the monies owed from the borrower's inheritance. But if there is no evidence of the debt and you neglect to make a Will, the borrower will receive whatever is allowed under the Rules Governing Intestate Succession.

That was the case with Sally and Tom and their four children. They were firm believers in treating each of their children equally. "Share and share alike" was their favorite saying. Once Tom died, Sally continued with the tradition.

Sally did not think of the loan she gave to her son as a gift. After all, he promised to pay it back, with interest! She did not ask her son to sign a promissory note. He was family. If you can't trust your son, who can you trust?

The son was prompt with his monthly payments. But only two payments had been made before his mother died suddenly, from a heart attack. Sally never mentioned the loan to any of her other children. Neither did her son.

Each child received one quarter of their mother's Estate; and no one the wiser. Except whenever Sally's son dreams of his mother, she is not smiling.

MAKE PROVISION FOR PAYMENT OF TAXES

Taxes are another concern for those Estates large enough to be subject to Estate Taxes. State and federal law require that Estate Taxes be paid by the beneficiaries of the Estate in proportion to the value received, unless the decedent made some other arrangements to pay for the taxes (Est. Powers & Trusts 2-1.8, 2-1.13). If you make no provision for the payment of taxes, whoever inherits your property will pay a percentage of the taxes based on the amount they receive.

Even property taxes that are assessed against real property owned by the decedent before his death must be paid by the beneficiary of the property (Surr. Ct. Proc. Act 1811).

If this is not as you wish you can direct your Personal Representative to pay all of your taxes from your Probate Estate. If you do so, beneficiaries of a specific gift, and those who inherit property from a Non-probate transfer will not contribute to the payment of your taxes. All of your taxes will be paid from your Probate Estate. This means that the amount that your residuary beneficiaries receive will be reduced by the amount of taxes paid.

MAKE PROVISION FOR PAYMENT OF DEBTS

Most Wills contain an instruction to the Personal Representative to ". . . pay all the expenses of my last illness, funeral expenses, costs of administration, taxes and just debts. . . " Under New York law, this instruction does not include paying off a loan on a gift made to a beneficiary. For example, if you have a loan on your car, the beneficiary of the car will inherit the loan along with the car unless you make specific provision in your Will for the loan to be paid from your Estate (Est. Powers & Trusts 3-3.6).

SET THE PERSONAL REPRESENTATIVE'S FEE

An important reason to make a Will is so that you can choose your Personal Representative and come to an understanding about how much compensation he is to receive. You can state that value in your Will. If you do not make provision for his fee, he is entitled to receive the amount as stated under New York law (Surr. Ct. Proc. Act 2307). As explained in Chapter 6, that fee is substantial. For example, the Personal Representative of an Estate worth $100,000 is entitled to $5,000 in commissions.

CAUTION THE PERSONAL REPRESENTATIVE CAN SEEK MORE MONEY

You can put the amount of agreed compensation in your Will; however your Personal Representative can reject that amount and ask for the amount allowed under law. To avoid the problem, you can have your attorney draft an Agreement that you and your Personal Representative sign and attach it to your Will. Having a separate fee Agreement will not stop your Personal Representative from asking for more money, but with such an Agreement, the Court will not agree to the increase unless something unusual occurs (such as a law suit) causing much more work than the ordinary Probate proceeding.

You also need to keep in mind that the Personal Representative's fee is just to administer the Estate. It does not include payment for professional work he may do while settling the Estate. For example, if you appoint your accountant to serve as Personal Representative, he is entitled to receive compensation for his work as Personal Representative and also for any accounting work he does such as preparing tax returns and providing an accounting for the beneficiaries.

A financial planner who serves as Personal Representative may be compensated for his management of the Estate property (buying and selling securities, taking care of rental property, etc.) in addition to his fee to administer the Estate.

The same goes for any other professional, such as your attorney. In fact, if you choose your attorney to serve as your Personal Representative, under New York law he must disclose to you that he is entitled to be paid as Personal Representative of your Estate and as the attorney for the Estate (Surr. Ct. Proc. Act 2307-a).

But the main problem with appointing a professional as your Personal Representative is the same as appointing a professional to serve as the Successor Trustee of your Trust; namely, that it creates a potential conflict of interest. The professional can use his position as Personal Representative to generate fees that may not have been necessary had someone else be settling the Estate.

When choosing a Personal Representative, consider the relationship of the Personal Representative to the beneficiaries and determine whether it would be better to appoint a non-professional for the job.

INCLUDE SAFEGUARDS FOR YOUR BENEFICIARIES

It is fairly common practice in New York, to include a waiver in the Will directing that the Personal Representative serve without bond. In general, the Court will respect you wishes and waive the bond requirement (Surr. Ct. Proc. Act 806). But keep in mind that your beneficiary is always free to sign his own waiver. If he feels comfortable that the Estate funds are safe, he can always ask the Court to waive bond.

CHOOSE A GUARDIAN FOR A MINOR CHILD

Each parent has the right to name someone in their Will to be Guardian of their child in the event that the parent dies before the child is grown, and the other parent is deceased. Should the surviving parent die, whoever the parent named to serve as Guardian will have priority to be appointed as Guardian of the minor child (Dom. Rel. 81).

It is important to choose someone who is compatible with your child, because if the child is 14 or older, the Judge will consider the child's choice of Guardian. He will give priority to the child's choice of Guardian, unless he finds that it is not in the child's best interest to appoint that person (C.P.L.R. 1210).

Some people think that preparing a Will is a simple thing — something they can do themselves. But writing a Will is like figure skating. It is harder than it looks. A Will needs to be clearly worded. A sentence that can be read in two different ways can lead to a dispute over what you intended; and that could result in a long and expensive Court battle. The Will must be signed and witnessed according to New York law, otherwise the Judge may refuse to admit the Will to Probate, and your property will be distributed as if you had no Will at all (Surr. Ct. Proc. Act 1408).

Unless you take the time to make yourself knowledgable about New York law as it relates to Wills, it is best to have an attorney who is experienced in Estate Planning, prepare one for you.

If the Will is not properly prepared and witnessed, the Judge may refuse to admit the Will to Probate, and your property will be distributed as if you had no Will at all.

As explained in Chapter 5, there are any number of reasons to challenge a Will. If you want to be assured that your Will is honored, it is best to have an Estate Planning attorney prepare a Will according to your directions and then supervise the signing of your Will. He will see to it that your Will is signed and witnessed in the presence of at least two disinterested witnesses — usually members of his staff. Each witness will sign a separate paragraph saying that they saw you sign the Will, and you did so of your own free will and at the time you signed it, you were competent to know what you were doing (Est. Powers & Trusts 3-2.1).

Once signed in this manner it will be difficult for anyone to say that you did not know what you were doing when you signed the Will. If your Will is challenged your attorney will be able to present proof to the Court that the Will was prepared exactly as you wished, and that you had full capacity when you signed the Will.

STORING THE WILL

Once you sign your Will, you may wonder where to store it. Your attorney may suggest that he place it in his vault for safekeeping. By doing so, he ensures that your heirs will need to contact him as soon as you die. This does not mean that they are required to employ him should a Probate proceeding be necessary. It only means that he will have an opportunity for future employment.

But there are problems with such an arrangement. The Will could be lost or mistaken for another Will. That happened in at least one case. The attorney prepared Wills for two people with the same name and similar family circumstances. When one person died the attorney submitted the wrong Will to Probate.

If you decided to allow your attorney to store the Will, you need assurances that the attorney will be responsible for the document. You should get a receipt and something in writing that says:

⇨ The attorney accepts full responsibility for the storage of the Will. Should it be lost or damaged, he will replace the document at no cost to you; and if you are deceased, he will, at no cost to your heirs, present sufficient evidence to the Court to accept a valid copy of the Will into Probate.

⇨ There will be no charge to you, or your heirs, for the storage and retrieval of the document.

⇨ Should he sell his practice, retire, or die, he or the successor to his practice, will return the original document to you.

THE SAFE DEPOSIT BOX — SAFE BUT . . .

You might consider placing your Will in a safe deposit box that you lease at a bank. The only problem with the bank safe deposit box is convenient access. If you hold a safe deposit box in your name only, should you die, the bank will not allow access to the box without an order from the Court. Once a Personal Representative is appointed, he will have authority to enter the box and remove its contents. But if you arranged your finances to avoid Probate, it is self defeating to have entry to a safe deposit box trigger a Probate procedure.

For those who are married, the solution to the problem of accessing the safe deposit box after death, is to lease the box jointly with your spouse, such that each of you has free access to the box. As explained in Chapter 7, those who have a Trust can solve the problem by giving their Successor Trustee joint access to the safe deposit box.

If you are single and do not have a Trust, you can lease the box jointly with a trusted family member. But, if privacy and security are important to you, this might offset any concern for the convenience of your beneficiaries.

Of course, you can always keep your Will in a fireproof safe in your home. Regardless of where you choose to store your Will, let your Personal Representative know that you have a Will and how to retrieve it in the event of your death.

CHOOSING THE RIGHT ESTATE PLAN

Joint Ownership?
An In Trust For Account?
A Transfer On Death Security?
A Trust?
A Will?
An Insurance Policy???

Chapters 7 and 8 offer so many options that the reader may be more confused than when he was blissfully unenlightened.

As with most things in life, you may find there are no ultimate solutions, just alternatives. The right choice for you is the one that best accomplishes your goal. This being the case, you first need to determine what you want to accomplish with the money you leave. Think about what will happen to your property if you were to die suddenly, without making any plan different from the one you now have.

> Who will be responsible to pay your bills?
> Who will get your property?
> Will Probate be necessary?

If the answers to these questions are not what you wish, then you need to work to arrange your property to accomplish your goals.

For those with significant assets — in particular, those with Estates large enough to pay Estate taxes, a trip to an experienced Estate Planning attorney may be well worth the consultation fee.

Your Estate Plan Record 9

Once you are satisfied with your Estate Plan, then the final thing to consider is whether your heirs will be able to locate your assets once you are gone.

Most people have their business records in one place, their Will in another place, car titles and deeds in still another place. When someone dies, their beneficiaries may feel as if they are playing a game of "hide and seek" with the decedent. The game might be fun were it not for the fact that an unlocated item may be forever lost. For example, suppose you die in an accident and no one knows you are insured by your credit card company for accidental death in the amount of $25,000. The only one to profit is the insurance company, which is just that much richer because no one told them that you died as a result of an accident.

And how about a key to a safe deposit box located in another state? Will anyone find it? Even if they find the key, how will they find the box?

It is not difficult to arrange things so that your affairs are always in order. It amounts to being aware of what you own (and owe) and keeping a record of your possessions. A side benefit is that by doing so, you will always know where all your business records are. If you ever spent time trying to collect information to file your taxes or trying to find a lost stock or bond certificate, you will appreciate the value of organizing your records.

ORGANIZING YOUR RECORDS

Heirs need all the help they can get. It is difficult enough dealing with the loss, without the frustration of trying to locate important documents. Your heirs will have no problem locating your assets if you keep all of your records in a single place. It can be a desk drawer or a file cabinet or even a shoe box. It is helpful if you keep a separate file or folder for each type of investment. You might consider setting up the following folders:

📁 THE BANK & SECURITIES FOLDER

Store your original certificates for stocks, bonds, mutual funds, certificates of deposit, in a folder labeled **BANK & SECURITIES FOLDER**. In addition to the original certificate include a copy of the contract you signed with each financial institution. The contract will show where you have funds and who you named as beneficiary or joint owner of the account. If someone owes you money and signed a promissory note or mortgage identifying you as the lender, store these documents in this folder as well.

If you have a safe deposit box, keep a record of its location and the number of the box. Keep a copy of all of the items stored in the box in this folder. If you have an extra key to the box, put it here.

E-bank Accounts If you are doing your banking on-line, it is important to keep a record of your passwords so that your family can access the account in the event of your incapacity or death. The same applies if you have on-line brokerage or installment loan accounts. Keep a paper record of these accounts in this folder.

📁 THE INSURANCE FOLDER

The INSURANCE FOLDER is for each insurance policy that you own, be it life insurance, car insurance, homeowner's insurance or a health care insurance policy. If you purchased real property, you probably received a title commitment at closing and the title insurance policy some weeks later when you received your original deed from recording. If you cannot locate the title insurance policy, contact the closing agent and have him send you a copy of your title policy.

📁 THE PENSION AND ANNUITY FOLDER

If you have a Pension or Annuity, then put all of the documents relating to the Pension in this folder. Include the telephone number and/or address of the person to contact in the event of your death.

FOR FEDERAL RETIREES If you are a Federal Retiree, you should have received your **PERSONAL IDENTIFICATION NUMBER (PIN)** and the person who will inherit your pension (your *survivor annuitant*) should have his/her own PIN as well. It is relatively simple to obtain this during your lifetime, but it may be difficult and/or stressful for your survivor annuitant to work through the system once you are gone.

Survivor annuitant benefits are not automatic. Your survivor annuitant must apply for them by submitting a death claim to the Office of Personnel Management. Your survivor needs to know that it is necessary to apply and also how to apply. You can get printed information about how to apply for benefits from the Office Of Personnel Management (see Page 32). Keep the printed information in this file.

🗀 THE DEED FOLDER

Many people save every scrap of paper associated with the closing of real property. If you closed recently on real estate and there was a mortgage involved in the purchase, you probably walked away from closing with enough paper to wallpaper your kitchen. If you wish, you can keep all of those papers in a separate file that identifies the property, for example:

CLOSING PAPERS FOR THE ROCHESTER PROPERTY

Place the original deed (or a copy if the original is in a safe deposit box) in a separate DEED FOLDER. Include cemetery deeds, condominium deeds, cooperative shares to real property, timesharing certificates, deed to out of state property, etc. Also include a copy of related documents such as an Abstract of Title, or a recorded Condominium Approval. If you have a title insurance policy, put the original in the insurance folder, and a copy in this folder. If you have a mortgage on your property, put a copy of the recorded mortgage and promissory note in a separate LIABILITY FOLDER.

LOCATING REAL PROPERTY

If you own a vacant lot, your beneficiaries will find the deed (or a copy) in this folder but that deed will not contain the address of that property because it doesn't have one. The post office does not assign a street address until there is a building on the site. Your beneficiaries can get the location of the property from city or county records. But why make things hard for them? Include a handwritten note in this folder that tells them exactly how to locate the property.

📁 THE LIABILITY FOLDER

The LIABILITY FOLDER should contain all loan documents of debts that you owe. For example, if you purchased real property and have a mortgage on that property, put a copy of the mortgage and promissory note in this folder. If you owe money on a car, put the loan documents in this folder. If you have a credit card, put a copy of the contract you signed with the credit card company in this folder. A lease is a liability, because you have contracted to pay a certain amount for the period of the lease, so include a copy of any lease agreement in this folder.

Many people never take the time to calculate their net worth (what a person owns less what that person owes). By having a record of your assets and outstanding debts, you can calculate your net worth whenever you wish.

📁 THE ESTATE PLANNING DOCUMENT FOLDER

Place your Estate Planning documents (Will, Trust, prenuptial agreement, burial, funeral arrangements, etc.) in a separate folder. If your attorney has your original documents, or you placed the original in a safe deposit box, place a copy of the document in this folder together with instructions about how to find the original. It is important to keep a copy of your Will or Trust because over the years you may forget what provision you made. Keeping a copy in your home may save you a trip to the safe deposit box to determine whether you need to update the document.

THE PERSONAL PROPERTY FOLDER

MOTOR VEHICLES

Put all motor vehicle titles in a Personal Property folder. This includes cars, mobile homes, boats, planes, etc. If you owe money on the vehicle, the lender may have possession of the title certificate. If such is the case, put a copy of the title certificate and registration in this folder and a copy of the loan documents in a separate liability folder.

If you own a boat or plane, identify the location of the motor vehicle. For example, if you are leasing space in an airplane hangar or in a marina, keep a copy of the leasing agreement in this file.

JEWELRY

If you own expensive jewelry, keep a picture of the item together with the sales receipt or written appraisal in this folder.

COLLECTOR'S ITEMS

If you own a valuable art or coin collection, or any other item of significant value, include a picture of the item in this file. Also include evidence of ownership of the item, such as a sales receipt or a certificate of authenticity, or a written appraisal of the property.

🗁 THE PERSONAL RECORDS FOLDER

The **PERSONAL RECORDS FOLDER** should include documents that relate to you personally, such as a birth certificate, naturalization papers, marriage certificate, divorce papers, military records, Social Security card, etc. If you have a Power of Attorney or a Health Care Proxy, you can place the document in this folder, or in your Estate Planning folder. If you placed the original document in a safe deposit box, keep a copy in this folder together with the location of the original.

🗁 THE TAX RECORD FOLDER

Your Personal Representative (or next of kin) will need to file your final income tax returns. Keep a copy of your tax returns (both federal and state) for the past three years in your Tax Record Folder.

As explained in Chapter 2, beginning in 2010, there will be a cap on the step-up basis to 4.3 million dollars for property inherited by the spouse and 1.3 million dollars for property inherited by anyone else. It is important to keep a record of the basis of your property, not only for your heirs, but for yourself should you decide to sell the property during your lifetime. If you purchase real property, you need to keep a record of the purchase price as well as monies you paid to improve the property. You will need these records to determine whether there will be a Capital Gains Tax on the transfer. Your accountant can help you set up a bookkeeping system to keep a running record of your basis in everything you own of value.

THE *If I Die* FILE

Many do not have the time, nor inclination, to "play" with all these folders. They do not anticipate an immediate demise. Getting hit by a truck, or dying in a fiery plane crash is not something to think about, much less prepare for. But consider that death is not the only problem. You could take suddenly ill (say with a stroke) and become incapacitated. Even the most time-starved optimist should have a murmur of concern that his loved ones will be left with a mess should something unforeseen happen.

If you do not feel like doing a complete job of organizing your records at this time, consider an abridged version. You can set up a single file with a list of all you own and the location of each item. You need to make that file easily accessible to whomever you wish to manage your affairs in the event of your incapacity or death. You can do this by letting that person know of the existence of the file and how to get it in an emergency; or keep the file in an easily accessible place in your home with the succinct but attention-grabbing title of *"If I Die."*

We have included a form on the next page that you can use as a basis for information to be included in the file.

If I Die

the following information will help settle my Estate:

INFORMATION FOR DEATH CERTIFICATE

MY FULL LEGAL NAME _____

MY SOCIAL SECURITY NO. _____

MY USUAL OCCUPATION _____

BIRTH DATE AND BIRTH PLACE _____

If naturalized, date & place _____

MY FATHER'S NAME _____

MY MOTHER'S MAIDEN NAME _____

PEOPLE TO BE NOTIFIED

_____

_____

_____

FUNERAL AND BURIAL ARRANGEMENTS

LOCATION OF BURIAL SITE

_____

LOCATION OF PREPAID FUNERAL CONTRACT

_____

FOR VETERAN or SPOUSE BURIAL IN A NATIONAL CEMETERY

BRANCH_____SERIAL NO._____

VETERAN'S RANK _____

VETERAN'S VA CLAIM NUMBER _____

DATE AND PLACE OF ENTRY INTO SERVICE:

_____

DATE AND PLACE OF SEPARATION FROM SERVICE:

_____

LOCATION OF OFFICIAL MILITARY DISCHARGE
OR DD 214 FORM_____

LOCATION OF LEGAL DOCUMENTS

BIRTH CERTIFICATE _____

MARRIAGE CERTIFICATE_____

DIVORCE DECREE _____

PASSPORT _____

WILL OR TRUST _____

DEEDS _____

MORTGAGES _____

TITLE TO MOTOR VEHICLES _____

HEALTH CARE DIRECTIVES _____

Attorney Name & Telephone   _____

LOCATION OF FINANCIAL RECORDS

INSURANCE POLICIES:

Name of Company, Location of Policy, Insurance Agent

_____

_____

PENSIONS/ANNUITIES:

IF FEDERAL RETIREE: PIN NUMBER: _____

NAME OF SURVIVOR _____

SURVIVOR PIN NUMBER _____

BANK

Name and address of Bank, Account Number,
Location of Safe Deposit Box and Key

_____

_____

SECURITIES

Name and telephone number of broker

_____

TAX RECORDS FOR PAST 3 YEARS

LOCATION _____

Name and telephone number of accountant

_____

KEEPING UP TO DATE

We discussed people's natural disinclination to make an Estate Plan until they are faced with their own mortality. Many believe that they will make just one Will and then die (maybe that's why they put off making a Will). The reality is, most people who make a Will change it at least once before they die. If you have an Estate Plan, it is important to update it when any of the following events take place:

✍ A CHANGE IN RELATIONSHIP

If you marry, divorce, have a child, or if a beneficiary of your Estate dies, you need to examine your Estate Plan to determine whether it needs to be revised. If you decide that your Will needs a complete revision, then have a new Will prepared. If you simply rip up the old Will, that will effectively revoke the Will. But it could happen that someone (perhaps your attorney) has a copy of the Will. If no one knows that you revoked the Will, they may think the Will is lost and then offer the copy of the Will for Probate (see page 81). If you draft a new Will, then the first paragraph should say, "I revoke all prior Wills ..."

BENEFICIARY MOVES OR DIES

Most people remember to name an alternate beneficiary should one of their beneficiaries die. But how many of us remember to notify the pension plan or insurance company when a beneficiary moves? Many life insurance proceeds are never paid because the company cannot locate the beneficiary. The Actuarial Office of the Federal Employees' Group Life Insurance Program reported that as of September, 2003, they had over 55.8 million dollars in unpaid benefits, mostly because they could not locate the beneficiary at the last given address.

✍ CHANGE IN MARITAL STATUS

Under New York law, should you divorce and die before you get around to changing your Will, any gift that you made in your Will or Trust for your former spouse is revoked. Your Probate Estate will be distributed as if your spouse died before you did. A legal separation in the state of New York does not end the marriage, so these laws do not apply to couples who are separated, legally, or otherwise (Est. Powers & Trusts 5-1.4). If you divorce (or even separate) it is important to review all of your Estate Planning documents (deeds, pension plans, insurance policies, Will or Trust etc.) to determine whether you wish to name a new beneficiary of your property.

NOTIFY EMPLOYER OF CHANGE

If you change your marital status (either marry or divorce) you need to tell your employer of the change so that the employer can change your status for purposes of paycheck tax deductions. If you have a health insurance plan or a pension plan, that provides benefits to your spouse or Domestic Partner, these need to be changed as well.

As explained in Chapter 6, New York law allows up to $30,000 of your property (final paycheck, bank or securities account, etc.) to be transferred to your spouse upon your death without going through Probate (Surr. Ct. Proc. Act 1310). If you change your marital status, you need to inform your employer, in writing, of the change. Ask your employer to put that writing in your work file.

✍ RELOCATION TO A NEW STATE OR COUNTRY

There is no need to change your Estate Plan for a move within the state of New York. There is much to check out if you are moving to another state. If your attorney has your original Will (or any other original document), then unless you plan to continue with him as your attorney, you need to retrieve those originals and take them with you to the new state.

You need to determine whether your Will conforms to the laws of the state of your new residence. Most states will honor a Will drafted according to New York law, however, the rights of a spouse vary considerably state to state. If you are married and have not provided the minimum amount as required by the laws of the new state, should you die before your spouse, your Will may be challenged on that basis. The same applies to a Trust. Many states, like New York, require funds from a Revocable Living Trust be used to pay the minimum amount allowed by law to the surviving spouse.

If you do not have a Will, then it is important to check out the Rules Governing Intestate Succession for that state. In some states they are called the *Laws of Descent and Distribution*. Each state has its own laws relating tthe inheritance of property and those laws are very different from each other. Who has the right to inherit your property in New York may be different from who will inherit your property in another state. If you do not have a Will, this is the time to think about who will inherit your property in the state of your new residence.

This is especially important for those who are married. The right of a spouse to inherit property varies significantly from state to state. There is a world of difference in the rights of a spouse in a Community Property state (Arizona, California, Idaho, Louisiana, Nevada, New Mexico, Texas, Washington and Wisconsin) and other states. There is even variation in the rights of a spouse from one Community Property state to another!

OTHER ESTATE PLANNING DOCUMENTS

Many states have laws directing physicians to honor a Health Care Directive that is properly drafted in another state. Other states will not recognize a Medical Directive unless it is drafted according to the laws of that state. But even if the laws of the state honor your New York Proxy and Living Will, consider drafting another in the new state. Medical Directives vary significantly state to state. Other states may have laws that enable you to appoint someone with powers similar to your Health Care Agent, but the laws of the state may refer to such person as a *Patient Advocate* or a *Health Care Surrogate* or a *Health Care Representative.*

It is best to sign a new Health Care Directive using the form and terminology recognized in the new state, rather than chance any confusion should you become ill and find yourself in an emergency situation. Similarly, if you have appointed someone to handle your finances under a Power of Attorney, you may want to have another prepared in conformity with the laws of the new state, so there will be no question of the right of your Agent to conduct business on your behalf.

CREDITOR PROTECTION

Creditor protection is another item that is significantly different state to state. If you have much debt, then determine what items can be inherited by your family free of your debts.

TAX CONCERNS

You also need to check out the taxes of the new state. Each state has its own tax structure. Some states have an inheritance tax, or a transfer tax on all inherited property. If state taxes are high, you may need an Estate Plan that will minimize the impact of those taxes.

When moving to another state you need to either educate yourself about the laws of the state, or consult with an attorney who can assist you in reviewing your Estate Plan to see if that plan will accomplish your goals in that state.

✍ A SIGNIFICANT CHANGE IN THE LAW

We pay our legislators (state and federal) to make laws and, if necessary, change those in effect. We pay judges to interpret the law and that interpretation may change the way the law operates. The legislature and the judiciary do their job and so laws change frequently. Tax laws are particularly volatile. The 2001 change in the federal Estate Tax law gradually increases the Exclusion amount so that by 2010 no Federal Estate Tax will be due regardless of the value of your Estate. You may be thinking that there is no need for an Estate Tax plan because you don't intend to die prior to 2010. But any certainty relating to death and taxes is false security (especially taxes, in this case). As explained in Chapter 2, the law as passed in 2001, is effective only until December 31, 2010. If lawmakers do nothing, then on January 1, 2011, the federal Estate Tax goes back into effect; and Estates that exceed one million dollars will once again be subject to Estate Taxes.

And that is not the only uncertainty. Each state has its own Estate Tax structure. It remains to be seen how each state will react to the position taken by the federal government in 2010. If federal Estate Taxes are phased out altogether, some states may follow the lead of the federal government and dispense with Estate Taxes. However, with states struggling to balance the budget, more likely they will see this as an opportunity to increase their Estate Taxes, so that Estate Taxes that would have been paid to the federal government will now be paid to the state.

You need to keep up with the news to learn about changes in the law that affect your Estate Plan. It is a good idea to check with your attorney on a regular basis to see if any change in the state or federal law affects your current Estate plan. And also check out the Eagle Publishing Company Web site for changes we will post to keep this book fresh. http://www.eaglepublishing.com

GAMES DECEDENTS PLAY

We discussed the game of "hide and seek" some decedents play with their heirs. A variation of that game is the "wild goose chase." The person who plays this game is one who never updates his files. His records are filled with all sorts of lapsed insurance policies, promissory notes of debts long since paid, brokerage statements of securities that have been sold, and so on.

When he is gone, his family will become frustrated as they try to hunt down the "missing" asset. If you want to play this game, the best joke is to keep the key to a safe deposit box that you are no longer leasing. That will keep folks hunting for a long time!

If you do not have a wicked sense of humor, do your family a favor and update your records on a regular basis.

Glossary

ABSTRACT OF TITLE An *Abstract of Title* is a condensed history of the title to the land. It consists of a summary of all the recorded documents that affect the land, including mortgages.

ADMINISTRATION The *Administration* of a Probate Estate is the management and settlement of the decedent's affairs. There are different types of administration. See ANCILLARY ADMINISTRATION.

AFFIANT An *Affiant* is someone who signs an affidavit and swears or acknowledges that it is true in the presence of a notary public or other person with authority to administer an oath or take acknowledgments.

AFFIDAVIT An *Affidavit* is a written statement of fact made by someone voluntarily, under oath, or acknowledged as being true, in the presence of a notary public or someone else who has authority to administer an oath or take acknowledgments.

AGENT An *Agent* is someone who is authorized by another (the principal) to act for or in place of the principal.

ANATOMICAL GIFT An *Anatomical Gift* is the donation of all or part of the body of the decedent for the purpose of transplantation or research.

ANCILLARY ADMINISTRATION An *Ancillary Administration* is a Probate proceeding that aids or assists the original (primary) Probate proceeding. Ancillary administration is conducted in another state to determine the beneficiary of the decedent's property located within that state, and to determine whether the property is taxable in that state.

ANNUAL GIFT TAX EXCLUSION The *Annual Gift Tax Exclusion* is the amount a person can gift to another each year without being required to file a federal Gift Tax Return. The Annual Gift Tax Exclusion is currently $11,000.

ANNUITANT   An *annuitant* is someone who is entitled to receive payments under an annuity contract.

ANNUITY An *annuity* is a contract that gives someone (the annuitant) the right to receive periodic payments (monthly, quarterly) for the life of the annuitant or for a given number of years.

ASSET An *asset* is anything owned by someone that has a value, including personal property (jewelry, paintings, securities, cash, motor vehicles, etc.) and real property (condominiums, vacant lots, acreage, residences, etc.).

ASSIGN To *assign* is to transfer one's rights to another; for example, a contract may allow the parties to assign their rights under the contract to another person,

ATTORNEY or ATTORNEY AT LAW An *attorney*, also known as an *Attorney at law*, or a *lawyer*, is someone who is licensed by the state to practice law in that state.

ATTORNEY-IN-FACT An *Attorney-In-Fact* is someone appointed to act as an Agent for another (the Principal) under a Power of Attorney.

BASIS The *basis* is a value that is assigned to an asset for the purpose of determining the gain (or loss) on the sale of the item or in determining the value of the item in the hands of someone who has received it as a gift.

BENEFICIARY A *beneficiary* is one who benefits from the act of another or from the transfer of property. In this book we refer to a beneficiary as someone named in a Will, Trust, or deed to receive property, or someone who inherits property under the Laws of Intestate Succession.

BOND A *bond* required by the Probate Court is a written document that guarantees the Personal Representative will perform his duties as required by law. The person or company that insures the performance of the Personal Representative is called a *surety.* The value of the bond is set by the Court. The cost of purchasing the bond is charged to the decedent's Estate.

CAPITAL GAINS TAX A *Capital Gains Tax* is a tax on the increase in the basis of property sold by a taxpayer.

CAVEAT *Caveat* is Latin for "Let him beware." It is a warning for the reader to be careful.

CFR *CFR* is the abbreviation for the *Code of Federal Regulations.*

CLAIM A *claim* against the decedent's estate is a demand for payment of a debt of the decedent. To be effective, the claim must be filed with the Probate Court within the time limits set by law.

CODE A *Code* is a body of laws arranged systematically for easy reference e.g. the Internal Revenue Code.

COLUMBARIUM A *Columbarium* is a vault with niches (spaces) for urns that contain the ashes of cremated bodies.

COMMISSIONER A *Commissioner* is someone appointed by the Court or by the government to do a job.

COMMON LAW MARRIAGE A *Common Law marriage* is one that is entered into without a state marriage license or any kind of official marriage ceremony. A Common Law marriage is created by an agreement to marry, followed by the two living together, and telling everyone they know that they are husband and wife. New York does not recognize a Common Law marriage unless it was entered into in another state that considers the union to be a valid marriage.

COMMUNITY PROPERTY   Certain states (Arizona, California, Idaho, Louisiana, Nevada, New Mexico, Texas, Washington, and Wisconsin) have laws stating that property acquired by husband or wife, or both, during their marriage is *Community Property* and is owned equally by both of them.

CONSERVATOR A *Conservator* is someone appointed by the Probate Court to manage, protect and preserve the property of someone who is missing, or who the Court finds is unable to care for his property because of age (a minor) or incapacity.

CONTINGENT BENEFICIARY A *Contingent Beneficiary* is an alternate beneficiary; i.e. someone who inherits if the primary beneficiary dies or loses the right to inherit.

CONFLICT OF INTEREST A *conflict of interest* is a conflict between the official duties of a fiduciary (Guardian, Trustee, attorney, etc.) and his own private interest. For example, it is a conflict of interest for a Successor Trustee to use Trust property for his own personal profit.

CONTRACT FOR DEED A *Contract for Deed* is essentially a mortgage. The seller of the property agrees to transfer title to the property (the deed) to the buyer once the buyer pays the amount agreed upon.

COOPERATIVE APARTMENT A *Cooperative Apartment* is an apartment in a complex in which each owner has an interest in the entire complex and a lease on his own apartment, although he does not own his apartment as in the case of the condominium. The complex is organized as a corporation. The ownership of a share in the corporation is considered to be personal property.

COURT The *Court* as used in this book is the Probate Court. When referring to an order made by the court, the term is synonymous with "judge," i.e., an "order of the court" is an order made by the judge of the court.

CREDITOR A *creditor* is someone to whom a debt is owed by another person (the *debtor*).

CREMAINS   *Cremains* is shorthand for *cremated remains*. It refers to the ashes of a person who was cremated.

CURTESY *Curtesy* is the right of a husband, upon the death of his wife, to a life estate in real property she owned during their marriage, provided they had a surviving child who could inherit the property. This English Common Law has been abolished in most states, including New York.

CUSTODIAN A *Custodian* under New York's *Uniform Transfers to Minors Act* is a person or a financial institution that accepts responsibility for the care and management of property given to a minor child.

DAMAGES *Damages* is money that is awarded by a Court as compensation to someone who has been injured by the action of another.

DEBTOR A *debtor* is someone who owes payment of money or services to another person (the *creditor*).

DECEDENT The *Decedent* is the person who died.

DEED OF TRUST A *Deed of Trust* is a deed that places title to real property in Trust to secure payment of monies owed on the property. It serves the same function as a mortgage.

DESCENDANT A *descendant* is someone who descends from a common ancestor. There are two kinds of descendants: a *lineal descendant* and a *collateral descendant*. The lineal descendant is one who descends in a straight line such as father to son to grandson. The collateral descendant is one who descends in a parallel line, such as a cousin. In this book, unless otherwise stated, the term *descendant* refers to a *lineal descendant*.

DEVISEE A *Devisee* is someone who inherits a gift of real property by Will.

DISTRIBUTION The *distribution* of a Trust or Probate Estate is the giving to the beneficiary that part of the Estate to which the beneficiary is entitled.

DOWER *Dower* is the right of a wife, upon the death of her husband, to a Life Estate in one-third of all real property that he owned during their marriage. This English Common Law has been abolished in most states, including New York.

ELECTIVE SHARE The *Elective Share* is the minimum amount of the decedent's Estate that a surviving spouse is entitled to receive under law. In New York, that amount is $50,000 or one-third of the decedent's *Net Estate*, whichever is greater. See NET ESTATE.

ENCUMBRANCE An *encumbrance* is a claim or a lien or a liability that is attached to real property, such as a mortgage, or lease or a mechanic's lien.

EQUITABLE *Equitable* is whatever is right or just. If property is distributed to two or more people equitably, then the division is not necessarily equal, but according to the principles of justice or fairness.

EQUITY The *equity* in a home is the market value of the home less monies owed on the property (mortgages, tax liens, etc.)

ESTATE A person's *Estate* is all of the property (both real and personal property) owned by that person. The decedent's estate may also be referred to as his *Taxable Estate* because all of the decedent's assets must be included when determining whether any Estate taxes are due after the person dies. Compare to Probate Estate.

EXECUTOR An *Executor* (feminine *Executrix*) is a legal term found in many Wills. The terms refer to the person appointed by the Will maker to carry out directions given in the Will.

FAMILY ALLOWANCE The *Family Allowance* is the amount set aside by the Probate Court to pay for the support and maintenance of the decedent's surviving spouse and dependents during the year following his death.

FIDUCIARY A *Fiduciary* is one who takes on the duty of holding property in Trust for another or acting for the benefit of another, such as a Personal Representative, Trustee, Guardian etc.. A fiduciary relationship is also one that is developed out of trust and confidence. For example, an attorney has a fiduciary relationship with his client.

GRANTEE   The *Grantee* of a deed is the person who receives title to real property from the *Grantor*.

GRANTOR The *Grantor* is someone who transfers property. The Grantor of a deed, is the person who transfers real property to a new owner (the Grantee). The Grantor of a Trust is someone who creates the Trust and then transfers property into the Trust. Also see *Settlor*.

GUARANTOR A *Guarantor* is someone who promises to pay a debt or perform a contract for another person in the event that person does not fulfill his obligation.

GUARDIAN A *Guardian* is someone who has legal authority to care for the person and/or property of a minor or for someone who has been found by the court to be incapacitated.

HEALTH CARE AGENT A *Health Care Agent* is someone who is appointed by another (the *Principal)* to authorize medical treatment for the Principal, in the event the Principal is to too ill to do so himself.

HEALTH CARE PROXY   A *Health Care Proxy* is a document in which a person appoints someone to serve as his Health Care Agent.

HOLOGRAPHIC WILL A *Holographic Will* is a Will written, dated and signed by the hand of the Will maker himself.

HOMESTEAD The *homestead* is the dwelling and land owned and occupied as the owner's principal residence.

HEIR   An *heir* is anyone entitled to inherit the decedent's property under the Rules Governing Laws of Intestate Succession in the event that the decedent dies without a Will.

INCAPACITATED   The term *incapacitated* is used in two ways. A person is *physically incapacitated* if he has a physical disability. A person is *legally incapacitated* if a court finds that a person is unable to care for his person or property. Once the Court determines that a person is legally incapacitated, the judge will appoint someone to care for the person or property of the incapacitated person.

INDIGENT   A person who is *indigent* is one who is poor and without funds.

IRA ACCOUNT An *Individual Retirement Account ("IRA")* is a retirement savings account in which income taxes on certain deposits and interest to the account are deferred until the monies are withdrawn.

IRREVOCABLE TRUST An *Irrevocable Trust* is a Trust that cannot be cancelled or terminated until its purpose is accomplished.

INSOLVENT A person or business is *insolvent* if more money is owed than owned, or if the person or business is unable to pay debts as they come due.

INTER VIVOS TRUST An *Inter Vivos Trust* (also known as a *Living Trust*) is a Trust that is created and becomes effective during the lifetime of the Grantor (or Settlor) as opposed to a Trust that he includes as part of his Will to take effect upon his death.

INTESTATE *Intestate* means not having a Will or dying without a Will. *Testate* is to have a Will or dying with a Will. See RULES GOVERNING INTESTATE SUCCESSION

ISSUE The decedent's *issue* are his descendants, children, grandchildren, great-grandchildren, etc. See DESCENDANT.

JOINT AND SEVERAL LIABILITY If two or more people agree to be *jointly and severally liable* to pay a debt, then each individually agrees to be responsible to pay the debt, and together they all agree to pay for the debt.

JOINT TENANCY In New York, a *Joint Tenancy* means that each Tenant owns an equal share of the property with right of survivorship; i.e., should one Joint Tenant die the remaining Tenant(s) own the property.

KEY MAN INSURANCE *Key man insurance* is an insurance policy designed to protect a company from economic loss in the event that an important employee of the company becomes disabled or dies.

KEOGH PLAN A *Keogh Plan* is a retirement plan available to self-employed taxpayers. Certain tax benefits are available such as tax deductions for annual contributions to the plan. The plan is named for its author, Eugene James Keogh.

LAWS OF DESCENT AND DISTRIBUTION See RULES GOVERNING INTESTATE SUCCESSION.

LEGALESE *Legalese* refers to the use of legal terms and confusing text that is used by some attorneys to draft legal documents.

LEGATEE A *Legatee* is a person to whom a legacy (gift) is given in a Will, as compared to an *Heir* who receives an inheritance under the Laws of Intestate Succession. For simplicity we have used the term *Beneficiary* for both Legatees and Heirs.

LESSOR A *Lessor* is a person or company who leases property to another (the *Lessee*). In the case of real property, the Lessor is known as the Landlord and the Lessee as the Tenant.

LETTERS *Letters* is a document, issued by the Probate court, giving the Personal Representative authority to take possession of and to administer the Estate of the decedent.

LIEN A *lien* is a charge against a person's property as security for a debt. The lien is evidence of the creditor's right to take the property as full or partial payment, in the event that the debtor defaults in paying the monies owed.

LIFE ESTATE A *Life Estate* interest in real property is the right to possess and occupy the property for so long as the owner of the Life Estate lives. When the owner of the Life Estate dies, the property will belong to the owner of the *Remainder Interest*.

LITIGATION *Litigation* is the process of carrying on a lawsuit, i.e., to sue for some right or remedy in a court of law. A Litigation Attorney is one who is experienced in conducting the law suit and in particular, going to trial.

LIVING WILL   A *Living Will* is a Health Care Directive that gives instructions about whether life support systems should be withheld or withdrawn in the event that the person who signs the Living Will is terminally ill or in a persistent vegetative state and unable to speak for himself.

MEDICAID *Medicaid* is a public assistance program sponsored jointly by the federal and state government to provide Medical Assistance for people with low income and limited assets.

NET ESTATE The *Net Estate* is defined by New York law to be the decedent's Probate Estate less funeral expenses, administrative expenses, and valid claims. It also includes Non-Probate transfers such as property held in the decedent's Trust, or in a joint account; as well as property gifted by the decedent at any time during his marriage for the benefit of anyone other than the surviving spouse.

NET PROCEEDS The *net proceeds* of a sale is the sale price less costs and expenses paid to make the sale.

NET WORTH A person's *net worth* is the value of all of the property that he owns less the monies he owes.

NEW YORK STATE SUPREME COURT *New York State Supreme Court* is a court of general jurisdiction, meaning that it has authority to hear cases and give judgments. The appellate division of the Supreme Court has authority to review decisions made in the Supreme Court.

NEXT OF KIN *Next of kin* has two meanings in law: *next of kin* refers to a person's nearest blood relation or it can refer to those people (not necessarily blood relations) who are entitled to inherit the property of a person who dies without a valid Will.

NON-PROBATE TRANSFER A *Non-probate Transfer* is the transfer of property to the decedent's beneficiary without the necessity of a Probate Procedure. This includes property that is transferred to the surviving joint owner, or property transferred to the beneficiary of an In Trust For accounts.

PERJURY *Perjury* is lying under oath. The false statement can be made as a witness in court or by signing an Affidavit. Perjury is a criminal offense.

PERSONAL EFFECTS *Personal effects* is personal property that is kept for one's personal use such as clothing, jewelry, books, and other items generally found in the home.

PERSONAL PROPERTY *Personal property* is all property owned by a person that is not real property (real estate). It includes personal effects, cars, securities, bank accounts, insurance policies, etc.

PERSONAL REPRESENTATIVE A *Personal Representative* is someappointed by the Probate Court to settle the decedent's Estate and to distribute whatever is left to the proper beneficiary.

PER STIRPES *Per Stirpes* is a method of distributing property to a group of beneficiaries. In the event a beneficiary dies before the gift is distributed, the deceased person's share goes to his descendants. If he has no descendants, the surviving beneficiaries share equally in the gift.

PETITION A *Petition* is a formal written, request to a Court asking the Court to take action or issue an order on a given matter; e.g. a request to appoint a Guardian.

POSTNUPTIAL AGREEMENT A *Postnuptial Agreement* is an agreement made by a couple after marriage to decide their respective rights in case of a dissolution or the death of a spouse.

POWER OF ATTORNEY A *Power of Attorney* is a document in which the person who signs the document (the *Principal*) gives another person (his *Agent*) authority to do certain things on behalf of the Principal.

PRENUPTIAL AGREEMENT A *Prenuptial Agreement* (also known as an *Antenuptial agreement*) is an agreement made prior to marriage whereby a couple determines how their property is to be managed during their marriage and how their property is to be divided should one die, or they later divorce.

PRINCIPAL The *Principal* of a Power of Attorney is the person who permits or directs another (his *Attorney-In-Fact* or *Agent*) to act for him.

PROBATE   *Probate* is a Court procedure in which a Court determines the existence of a valid Will. The Decedent's Estate is then settled by the Personal Representative who pays all valid claims and then distributes whatever remains to the proper beneficiary.

PROBATE ESTATE The *Probate Estate* is that part of the decedent's Estate that is subject to Probate. It includes property that the decedent owned in his name only or as a Tenant In Common. It does not include property that was held jointly with right of survivorship. It does not include property held in trust for someone.

PRO BONO The term *Pro Bono* means "for the public good." When an attorney works Pro Bono, he does so voluntarily and without pay.

PUNITIVE DAMAGES *Punitive damages* are awarded by a Court to punish someone who deliberately disregarded the rights or safety of another. It is money awarded in addition to *compensatory damages* which are monies awarded to reimburse the wronged person for actual losses.

REAL PROPERTY *Real property,* also known as *real estate,* is land and anything permanently attached to the land such as buildings and fences.

REMAINDER INTEREST The *Remainder Interest* in real property is the property that passes to the owner of that Interest, once the owner of the Life Estate dies. See LIFE ESTATE

RESIDENT AGENT A *Resident Agent* of a corporation is some-one who is authorized to act on behalf of the company and accept service of process in the event the company is sued.

RESIDUARY BENEFICIARY A *residuary beneficiary* of a Will is a beneficiary who is entitled to whatever is left of the Probate Estate once specific gifts made in the Will have been distributed and once the decedent's bills, taxes and costs of probate have been paid. If there is more than one residuary beneficiary, then unless the Will states differently they share equally in the Residuary Estate.

RESIDUARY ESTATE A *Residuary Estate* is that part of a Probate Estate that is left after all expenses and costs of administration have been paid and specific gifts have been distributed.

REVOCABLE TRUST A *Revocable Trust* is a Trust which can be amended or revoked by the Grantor or Settlor during his lifetime.

REVOCABLE LIVING TRUST A *Revocable Living Trust* (also known as an *Inter Vivos Trust*) is a Revocable Trust that is created and becomes effective during the lifetime of the Grantor or Settlor.

RULES GOVERNING INTESTATE SUCCESSION *The Rules Governing Intestate Succession* are the laws of the state relating to who is entitled to inherit the decedent's Probate Estate when he dies without a valid Will. In some states they are referred to as the *Laws of Descent.*

SECURED LOAN A *Secured loan* is a loan backed by property. If the borrower does not pay the debt, the lender can take the property. Car loans and mortgages are secured loans.

SELF PROVED WILL A *Self Proved Will* is a Will that eliminates some of the formalities of proof in a Probate procedure. The Will is made Self Proved by an Affidavit, signed by the witnesses, in the form as required by the statute.

SETTLOR A *Settlor* or *Trustor* is someone who creates a Trust.

SHORT CERTIFICATE A *Short Certificate* is a document issued by the Probate Court giving the Voluntary Administrator authority to conduct a Summary Procedure.

SIBLING A *sibling* is one of two or more people born of the same parents; i.e., a brother or a sister. Unless, otherwise noted, we used the term to include those who have only one parent in common; i.e. a half brother or a half sister.

SOLEMNIZE To *solemnize* a marriage is to enter a marriage publicly, before witnesses, rather than privately as in a common law marriage.

SPECIFIC GIFT A *Specific Gift* is a gift of a specific item, or part of the Will maker's Estate, that is made to a named beneficiary of the Will.

SPENDTHRIFT A *spendthrift* is someone who spends money carelessly or wastefully or extravagantly.

SPENDTHRIFT TRUST A *Spendthrift Trust* is a Trust created to provide monies to a beneficiary, and at the same time protect the Trust property from being taken by the creditors of the beneficiary.

STATUTE OF LIMITATION A *Statute of Limitation* is a federal or state law that sets maximum time periods for taking legal action. Once the time set out in the statute passes, no legal action can be taken.

STEPPED-UP BASIS A *stepped-up basis* is the fair market value placed on property that is purchased or inherited from another. The "step-up" refers to the increase in value from the basis of the former owner (usually what he paid for it), to the basis of the new owner (usually the market value when the transfer is made).

SUCCESSOR TRUSTEE A *Successor Trustee* is someone who takes the place of the Trustee.

SUMMARY PROCEDURE A *Summary Procedure* is a simplified and/or shortened Probate procedure.

SURROGATE A *Surrogate* is a substitute; someone who acts in place of another.

TENANCY BY THE ENTIRETY   A *Tenancy by the Entirety* is the name of a form of ownership of real property held by a husband and wife. It is a joint tenancy with right of survivorship, modified by the common law concept that the husband and wife are one. With a joint tenancy with right of survivorship, each joint tenant owns their own share of the property until death, when the surviving owner owns it 100%. With a Tenancy by the Entirety, each owns 100% of the property both before and after death.

TENANCY IN COMMON   *Tenancy In Common* is a form of ownership such that each tenant owns his/her share without any claim to that share by the other tenants. Unlike a joint tenancy, there is no right of survivorship. Once a tenant in common dies, his/her share belongs to the tenant's estate and not to the remaining owners of the property.

TESTATE *Testate* means having made a Will or dying with a Will.

TESTATOR The *Testator* is someone who makes and signs a Will; or someone who dies leaving a Will.

TITLE INSURANCE   *Title Insurance* is a policy issued by a title insurance company after searching title to the property. The insurance covers losses that result from a defect of title, such as unpaid taxes, or a claim of ownership of the property.

TRUST AGREEMENT A *Trust Agreement* is a document in which someone (the Grantor, Settlor or Trustor) creates a Trust and appoints a Trustee to manage property placed into the trust. The usual purpose of the Trust is to benefit persons or charities named by the Grantor as beneficiaries of the Trust.

TRUSTEE A *Trustee* is a person, or institution, who accepts the duty of managing Trust property for the benefit of another.

UNDUE INFLUENCE *Undue influence* is pressure, influence or persuasion that overpowers a person's free will or judgment, so that a person acts according to the will or purpose of the dominating party.

VOLUNTARY ADMINISTRATOR A *Voluntary Administrator* is someone who is appointed by the Probate Court to be in charge of settling the decedent's Estate by means of a Summary Procedure.

WAIVER A *waiver* is the intentional and voluntary giving up of a known right.

WARRANTY DEED A *Warranty Deed* is a deed in which the Grantor warrants (promises) that the property he is transferring has good and clear title; i.e., that no one else has rights in the property. This is different than a *Quit-claim Deed* where the Grantor says, in effect, "I am releasing any interest I have in this property to you, but I make no guarantees about anyone else's right to this property."

WRONGFUL DEATH A *wrongful death* is a death that was caused by the willful or negligent act of a person or company.

INDEX

A

WEB SITES

NEW YORK WEB SITES

149 New York Statutes are referenced in
Guiding Those Left Behind In New York

Each state has its own set of laws relating to the settlement of a person's Estate. The laws that are referenced in this book are very different from the laws of other states.

The author is in now in the process of "translating"
Guiding Those Left Behind
for the rest of the states, that is, writing state specific books that explain how to settle the affairs of someone who dies in the given state.

Books for the following states are now in print:
ALABAMA, ARIZONA, CALIFORNIA, CONNECTICUT
FLORIDA, GEORGIA, HAWAII, ILLINOIS, INDIANA
IOWA, KENTUCKY, LOUISIANA, MASSACHUSETTS
MARYLAND, New York, MINNESOTA, MISSOURI
MISSISSIPPI, NEW JERSEY, NEW YORK
NORTH CAROLINA, OHIO, OKLAHOMA
PENNSYLVANIA, SOUTH CAROLINA, TENNESSEE
TEXAS, UTAH, VIRGINIA, WASHINGTON, WISCONSIN

Readers of this book can purchase *Guiding Those Left Behind* for $22. This includes shipping.

To order or to check for book availability in other states call Eagle Publishing Company at (800) 824-0823.
- or -
Visit our Web site http://www.eaglepublishing.com

BOOK REVIEWS OF *Guiding Those Left Behind*

ARIZONA

Ben T. Traywick of the Tombstone Epitaph said "This book is an excellent reference book that simplifies all the necessary tasks that must be done when there is a death in the family. There is even an explanation as to how you can arrange your own estate so that your heirs will not be left with a multitude of nagging problems." "The reviewer has been going through probate for two years with no end yet in sight. This book at the beginning two year ago would have helped immensely."

CALIFORNIA

Margot Petit Nichols of the Carmel Pine Cone called it a ". . .TRULY RIVETING READ." " . . . I could scarcely put it down." "This is a book that we should all have, either on our book shelves or thoughtfully placed with our important papers."

FLORIDA

Maryhelen Clague of the Tampa Tribune Times wrote "Amelia Pohl has created a handy, self-help guide that illustrates the necessary steps that must be taken when someone dies, a guide that is easy to read, extremely clear and simple to refer to when the need arises."

NEW YORK

Saul Friedman of NEWSDAY said "And one section that should be read by readers of any age, suggests and describes how to create an 'If I Die' file to point the way to your vital papers and policies, to minimize the problems and costs for your survivors. Alas, not even you boomers will live forever."

OTHER BOOKS BY AMELIA E. POHL

How To Defend Yourself Against Your Lawyer

is a book about the unhappy experiences people have with their lawyers, beginning with that of the author AMELIA E. POHL. She became involved in a law suit and found herself in the role of client, rather than lawyer. She become concerned with lawyers who do not provide their clients with the loyalty and respect they deserve. This book is a result of those concerns.

The book is divided into chapters that cover the most common problems that take people to a lawyer: divorce, probate, criminal, personal injury, starting a business, making a Will, buying a house, etc. Each chapter tells of the misadventures of the unwary as they sought the services of a lawyer without a clue as to what they were "buying." This book is funny, sad, interesting, but most of all informative. It tells the reader how to become a savvy consumer, i.e., how to find the right lawyer for the right job. If the reader ever finds the need to employ a lawyer, he will be glad he read this book.

Copyright 2004   272 pages 6" X 9" soft cover
$20 includes Shipping and Handling

Beyond Grief To Acceptance and Peace

AMELIA E. POHL and the noted psychologist BARBARA J. SIMMONDS, Ph.d, have written a book for those families who have suffered a loss.

What to say to the bereaved

✧ How to help a child through the loss

✧ Strategies to adjust to a new life-style

✧ When and where to seek assistance.

80 pages   6" X 9" $10 includes Shipping and Handling

A Will is Not Enough. . .

Many people who have a Will think that they have their affairs in order. They believe that their Will can take care of any problem that may arise. But the primary function of a Will is to distribute property to people named in a Will. A Will cannot:

⇨ Protect your assets and limit your debt

⇨ Provide care for a minor or disabled child

⇨ Avoid Guardianship

⇨ Appoint someone to make your health care decisions should you be unable to do so

⇨ Appoint someone to handle your finances should you be unable to do so

⇨ Arrange to pay for your health care should you need long term nursing care, including qualifying for MEDICAID.

AMELIA E. POHL, Esq. has written a series of state specific books explaining how to do all of these things. This new book series is a continuation of this book. It builds on basic Estate Planning concepts introduced in Chapter 7 of this book and then goes on to introduce other, more sophisticated, Estate Planning methods. Although the topics are sophisticated, the writing style is the same as in this book. It is written in plain English. It is intended for use by the average person.

A Will Is Not Enough is now available for:

ARIZONA, CALIFORNIA, CONNECTICUT, FLORIDA
GEORGIA, HAWAII, INDIANA, ILLINOIS, MARYLAND
MASSACHUSETTS, NEBRASKA, NEW JERSEY
NEW MEXICO, NEW YORK, OREGON, PENNSYLVANIA
TEXAS, VIRGINIA, WASHINGTON, WISCONSIN

Readers of this book can purchase *A Will Is Not Enough* for $25. To check for book availability in other states call Eagle Publishing Company at (800) 824-0823.

It is the goal of EAGLE PUBLISHING COMPANY to keep our publications fresh.

As we receive information about changes to the federal or state law we will post an update to this edition at our Web site.

http://www.eaglepublishing.com